"As passionate about empowering the next generation as she is about leading hers, Darlene Zschech is possibly the most amazing mentor I know. Who better to learn from than Darlene, who continues to raise up in her wake some of the most influential, inspiring, and imaginative leaders on the face of the planet. She has lived this book so well. Let her lead you and equip you to release others."

—LOUIE GIGLIO
The Passion Movement/Passion City Church

"Great leaders like Darlene Zschech pour themselves into others. Packed with valuable, practical insights, this passionate and powerful book calls established and rising leaders to work together, showing how they can combine their unique strengths to leave an even greater legacy for the generations to come."

—JOHN C. MAXWELL
Bestselling author, speaker, and founder of
The John Maxwell Company

"When you get to know Darlene you understand that she loves people. Not just the 'shiny' people you would expect to circulate in her world, but the broken, the poor, and the downhearted. I've seen her time and time again encourage people who no one else would believe in. Many of these are now well-known names on the worship circuit who started life very differently but she saw potential in them. This book will help us all to understand that the gospel is about people not a brand."

—MARTIN SMITH
Songwriter, former lead singer of Delirious?, and
founder of CompassionArt

Books by Darlene Zschech

The Art of Mentoring
Extravagant Worship
The Kiss of Heaven
Revealing Jesus

DARLENE ZSCHECH is acclaimed worldwide as a singer, songwriter, worship leader, and speaker—most notably for her involvement in the music from Hillsong Church over many years. Although she has achieved numerous gold albums and her songs are sung in many nations, her success stands as a testimony to her life's passion to serve God and people with all her heart.

Mark and Darlene's life commitment to do whatever they can to bring answers and relief to human suffering prompted the birth of HOPE: Rwanda to bring hope and healing to that nation seemingly forgotten since the genocide of 1994. As this HOPE has spread into Cambodia, Vanuatu, India, Uganda, and beyond, their work through HOPE: Global continues to gather momentum. They also actively work with Compassion International serving the world's poorest children.

In 2011, Mark and Darlene became senior pastors of Hope Unlimited Church on the beautiful Central Coast of New South Wales, where they now live with their family. While they travel extensively and have the honor of ministering around the globe, Darlene says, "First and foremost I am a woman who simply and wholeheartedly loves Christ, and serves Him through loving my family, serving the church, and speaking up for those who cannot speak for themselves."

For more information, visit *darlenezschech.com* and *hopeunlimitedchurch.com*.

DARLENE ZSCHECH

THE ART
OF MENTORING

EMBRACING THE GREAT
GENERATIONAL TRANSITION

BETHANYHOUSEPUBLISHERS

a division of Baker Publishing Group
Minneapolis, Minnesota

© 2009, 2011 by Darlene Zschech
Extravagant Worship, Inc.
Edited by Karen Kaufman

Some material in this book appeared previously in *The Great Generational Transition*, EWI Inc., Baulkham Hills NSW 2153, Australia.

Published by Bethany House Publishers
11400 Hampshire Avenue South
Bloomington, Minnesota 55438
www.bethanyhouse.com

Bethany House Publishers is a division of Baker Publishing Group, Grand Rapids, Michigan.

Printed in the United States of America

ISBN 978-0-7642-0935-2

The Library of Congress has cataloged the hardcover edition as follows:
Zschech, Darlene.
    The art of mentoring : embracing the great generational transition / Darlene Zschech.
        p. cm.
Summary: "An internationally known singer and worship leader discusses how both the rising and established generations of local church leadership can and should work together"—Provided by publisher.
        Includes bibliographical references (p.   ).
        ISBN 978-0-7642-0934-5 (hardcover : alk. paper)
        1. Christian leadership. 2. Mentoring in church work. 3. Intergenerational relations—Religious aspects—Christianity. I. Title.
        BV652.1.Z83 2011
        253—dc23   2011019419

Unless otherwise identified, Scripture quotations are from the HOLY BIBLE, NEW INTERNATIONAL VERSION®, NIV®, Copyright © 1973, 1978, 1984 by Biblica, Inc.™ Used by permission of Zondervan. All rights reserved worldwide. www.zondervan.com

Scripture quotations identified AMP are taken from the Amplified Bible, copyright © 1954, 1958, 1962, 1964, 1965, 1987 by The Lockman Foundation. Used by permission.

Scripture quotations identified THE MESSAGE are from THE MESSAGE by Eugene H. Peterson, copyright © 1993, 1994, 1995, 2000, 2001, 2002. Used by permission of NavPress Publishing Group. All rights reserved.

Page 192 is a continuation of the copyright page.

Cover design by Lookout Design, Inc.
Cover photograph © Aflo Sport / Masterfile

Interior design by Melinda Schumacher
Interior photographs: Shutterstock.com

To
my own children,
Amy, Chloe, and Zoe Jewel,
whose lives inspire me to live
with joy and purpose—
their future my greatest motivator,
their "dreams come true"
my greatest prayer.

*Watch what God does, and then
do it, like children who learn proper
behavior from their parents. Mostly
what God does is love you. Keep company with him and learn a life of love.
Observe how Christ loved us. His love was
not cautious but extravagant. He didn't
love in order to get something from us
but to give everything of himself to
us. Love like that.*

—*Ephesians 5:1–2*
THE MESSAGE

CONTENTS

FOREWORD

It is always significant when someone fully in touch with the church globally speaks into the present moment.

Darlene Zschech is such a person, and thankfully she is intensely practical.

Darlene is not only an influencer of the global church worship life through her music and gifting, she is also an experienced pastoral leader and a respected voice to today's youth culture. Further, she is a faithful wife and an effective mother; she and her husband, Mark, have three daughters, one son-in-law, and two grandbabies.

So it is without reserve, in this book you have in your hands there is workable wisdom from a woman who qualifies to be heard by all of us.

My respect for the writer transcends her remarkable personal gifts. It is prompted by the clear-headedness, the Word-centeredness, and Christ-consciousness that she evidences.

Whether you encounter her as a worship leader, hear her as an internationally welcomed speaker, or converse with her as I often have as a friend, you encounter genuine sincerity, spiritual substance, and personal graciousness.

I've listed the above six qualities about Darlene not only

because they're true of her but also because they are so necessary to each of us today. They are values that must be relayed and reinforced—traits needful of transmission to a rising generation by mentors and models living them as they help serve and shape the younger ones who are watching and following us.

I think you'll find "fresh air" within these pages—a breath of insight and inspiration to increase your sensitivities and response to these remarkable times.

Societal change is so rapid that without the balance and weight added by those with discerning perspective, confusion and deception are a constant threat. That's why I'm thankful for the content here. It will help each of us to perceive and address the moment—adding balance and weight to our own experience, enriching our own potential for investing it in those we are called by God to help rise to their own life-purpose.

Whether you're a part of the rising generation, or one of those called to welcome and assist it to its potential for making an eternal difference in our world, join me in responding to its message.

Tune in to the times being addressed by this prophetic message at this pivotal moment.

The message is clear: It's ours to hear.

And to take action—now!

Jack W. Hayford
Founding Pastor, The Church On The Way
Founder-Chancellor, The King's University

INTRODUCTION:
THE WHY AND THE WHAT

A good place to start . . .

Psalm 145:3–7: "God is magnificent; he can never be praised enough. There are no boundaries to his greatness. Generation after generation stands in awe of your work; each one tells stories of your mighty acts. Your beauty and splendor have everyone talking; I compose songs on your wonders. Your marvelous doings are headline news; I could write a book full of the details of your greatness. The fame of your goodness spreads across the country; your righteousness is on everyone's lips" (THE MESSAGE).

If these words from David the psalmist sound a bit like the adventure you want to experience and share with the next generation, then keep on reading, my friend!

My story in ministry thus far has been one of the greatest adventures ever. As often happens in life, occasionally it's been a bumpy course with some very hard times—but the sweetness of Jesus has by far superseded any pain, so I wouldn't trade a moment of it. And though I could never compose enough songs to include all His wonders, or write a book worthy of His greatness, I do want to share as practically and honestly as I can some of the hurdles encountered in my endeavor to mentor the next generation. As you read this book, I pray that you too will be equipped by God's grace to walk into future seasons of transitioning leadership with kindness and great strength.

Mark and I and our family have for many years been honored to be part of Hillsong Church in Sydney, Australia, where leadership is modeled and encouraged, and where corporate mentoring and making a place for the next generation has always been utmost in priority and strategy.

— So this is my frame of reference: doing life as a team of leaders whose life passion is to take a journey into the heart of God and to discover the true meaning of worship. I have personally worked hard at developing my own leadership abilities—sitting under great teaching, reading voraciously, listening with both my head and my heart, and observing those I want to emulate.

And this is what I know to be true: If life were merely about our personal sense of fulfillment, then much of this book would be unnecessary—but because you and I are called to follow the great example of Jesus Christ, who came to this earth to live and die for people, and to change us by His grace into a family who can love like He loves, I feel compelled to share what is on my heart. It is my deepest desire to remind leaders everywhere that the kingdom of God is about people and that we are not here to build our own kingdoms but to bring God's kingdom into the lives of others. A life lived in Christ is a sacrificial life—a life poured out, a life lived to lift the lives of others.

As I've chatted with leaders on my travels throughout the globe, I have discovered that the art of mentoring and guiding teams through the maze of transition, both corporately and individually, is not about teaching *me*ology. It is found in helping others to reach their full potential so they can know, appreciate, and use the great heritage of the faith available in Christ.

From the moment I stepped into my local church as a tentative fifteen-year-old, I had the sense of coming home. And it was this open-armed welcome that made me love the house of God. Even as I've grown and become more familiar with what His house and His people represent, I have come to value and appreciate the presence of God in His sons and daughters in a completely sacred and tender way.

And because I have felt so readily received as a disciple of Christ, who was always willing in heart but very broken in soul, I am now passionate about extending love and acceptance to this generation and the generations to come. I want people everywhere to experience a strong and powerful understanding of who each one is in Christ and how valuable and needed every one of us is *right now*.

But in saying all that, as I've journeyed through church life, I've seen that there exists a great divide when it comes to one generation being even aware of the next. I've spoken to many leaders who have outstanding dedication to the things of God and yet seem to lack revelation about raising the next generation to serve Him. Some well-meaning leaders do not see their responsibility to evoke and encourage new ways and fresh ideas from those who may be decades younger. But the truth is that as fathers and mothers in the Lord, it is our responsibility to help our sons and daughters to achieve more than we could ever have dared to dream so that one generation can build upon the next. With that said, this book does not say to anyone who may feel older or out of date that your time is over or that it's time to step aside.

On the contrary, this book was written to give you tools to empower those God has entrusted to you for the purpose of mentoring—and to give you a little well-worn information that might save you a whole lot of heartache in the future!

So I pray that you will hear my heart in these pages and learn from my journey—mistakes and all—so you too will find that when you pour yourself into seeing the dreams of others come true, the Lord will bring to pass some of your own unrealized dreams.

Psalm 37:4 says, "Take delight in the LORD, and he will give you the desires of your heart." This verse became a reality for me a couple of years ago when I had the opportunity to meet the great John Maxwell, a leadership teacher who has had a major influence on my life. I had come with a specific question for him, and I wanted to hear his wisdom regarding raising strong leadership generationally. I wanted to glean from his experience in ministry, in family, and in business, so I asked him about mentoring and generational transition. He said, "Unless the *why* behind the *what* is taught consistently—unless we preach a standard and not just a method—then yes, clarity, precision, and, most important, the original *why* becomes very distorted amidst all the doing what we do."

Even though I have much growing to do in every area of my own life, I am convinced that this generation of worshipers and leaders wants to be involved with a message that moves people to the core of their being. They are not interested in giving their lives to passive, plastic melodies or mundane methods of worship. They don't want to "pretend" to know God, they want the real thing. I know firsthand that once you've tasted the reality of God—not hype or excitement, but the great filling of His glory through your veins—your spiritual taste buds are simply ruined for anything counterfeit.

There is no substitute for His presence, for it is there that we behold His glory and we are changed. It is His presence that I want you to experience as you read.

I have endeavored to keep this book strong and yet practical; therefore, rather than creating chapters, I've called each section a *value*. These topics are critical in preparing the ground for a successful shift, whether large or small. The sections are in no particular order, and some values may apply to your situation more than others.

However, as you read, I pray that you will consider Psalm 145 and how this Scripture might become a reality in your own day-to-day environs. My hope is that this book will fuel a commitment to achieving your full potential and possibilities in Christ and that you will use those strengths to make a way for the next generation.

Whether you are part of a local church that is embracing change or one that is resisting on all sides, whether you live in a country that is in the early development stages or one that may have more immediate access to funding and opportunity, I can assure you that the Word of God works wherever it is applied.

Let's take the journey together and master the art of mentoring so that we might create a seamless generational transition . . .

I *so* believe in you.

VALUE **ONE:**
TIME FOR GROWTH

A Message from God-of-the-Angel-Armies: "Old men and old women will come back to Jerusalem, sit on benches on the streets and spin tales, move around safely with their canes—a good city to grow old in. And boys and girls will fill the public parks, laughing and playing—a good city to grow up in."
—Zechariah 8:4–5
THE MESSAGE

In any season where transition is required, a growth phase happens that is critical to both the mentor and the mentee. We all need "a good city to grow old in . . . a good city to grow up in." Whether we are looking for a place to call home, where we can tell our experiences about God's goodness, or just beginning the process of growing up and looking for a place to laugh and play with peers, we are all in the process of growing.

And with that growth comes the pain of stretching and changing—but take heart, growing pains are normal and necessary. Anything worth achieving in this life requires time, patience, and some discomfort. For example, we look at the words of the psalmist and think, *If only I could express my heart with so much transparency. If only I could trust and believe with the wholehearted assurance that he had.* What we forget is the amount of time it took to develop that kind of trust. We overlook the fact that David the psalmist spent a lifetime putting his words on paper and learning how to let his heart be exposed and matured before the Lord.

David often cried out to heaven, "How long?" These two words are common to each of us as we struggle to experience answers to prayer. We wonder as we plead our case: *How long must I wait until the hand of God steps into my reality to bring the miracle that only He can supply? How long until this situation turns around? How long until these questions in my heart are answered? How long until the people who have dismissed me will finally hear?*

How long? It's been an all-too-familiar question in my life.

So many times I have asked, "How long will it take for us as leaders and friends to realize that it is our responsibility to pass on what we know and to empower those growing up behind us— whether they are our natural children or those in our sphere of leadership and influence." I have a burning desire to see the fruits of one generation being passed to the next so that the younger can learn from the older.

My grandparents are a living example of this section's opening Scripture. My grandfather, known as Pop in our family, is ninety-nine years old. He and my Nan have been blessed with exceptional health, and at the time of this writing live independently, loving God, loving each other, and loving and serving in their local church. They are a shining example of people whose stance is poised to serve others. On countless occasions, people have told me of a time when Nan and Pop opened their home to them or to someone they knew. My grandparents shared their food, resources, and wisdom whenever possible, continually pouring themselves out to be a blessing to someone else. Above all, what stands out is their unwavering commitment to encourage and inspire the younger generations. They have been unwavering in *telling us the stories* of God's faithfulness throughout their lifetime, encouraging us in our faith and helping us to see that God will be true to His Word no matter how difficult the situation may look today.

Just a few weeks ago, Mark and I went over to Nan and Pop's to share what we sensed God was saying about our next season. And like the faithful man of God that he is, Pop laid his hands on our heads and prayed a mighty prayer of faith, asking God to release His favor over his children so that the handiwork of Christ would be seen in our lives in unprecedented measure. The presence of Almighty God in that moment was overwhelming.

Later, Mark and I discussed how deeply moved we were by Pop's passion to see God's Word and power established in our lives. Pop has told us story after story of how God delivered Nan and him, each time reminding us that if God could do it then, He can do it now. We are so thankful to have his influence in our lives.

You might be thinking, Well, I don't have grandparents in the Lord who share their stories with me, and I don't have anyone to release a blessing over my generation. Dear friend, that void is the point of this writing. You can become for others what you did not have so that the generation following you will have your "faith stories" to lean on and your blessing to pass along. As you step into roles of leading people in your daily routines, I pray that your earnest desire will be to see the next generation inspired, focused, and filled with compassion for the lost and the broken. You and I can be the difference that changes the future. Let me encourage you: Tell your stories . . . so that the rich history of the miraculous is continually brought front and center. In so doing, you will give the next generation strength to hang on!

You Have Influence

I know that you are a believer who is longing to have influence—and you do. The hearts of people throughout the earth are stirring, and more than ever, people are looking for change. We are living in exciting times, and I am just crazy enough to believe that we are about to see a great global revolution within the body of Christ. I also believe that you and I actually have a dynamic part to play in it. We are living in the times that those who preceded us diligently prayed about, dreamed about, and bravely pioneered. Over time, they have laid a foundation and paid the price for the increased level of unity we now experience in the church. The result has been a growing and worldwide Spirit-fueled passion to relieve human suffering.

⁓ Faith is rising and hope remains strong, even though the state of humanity is in dire need, and the church—as beautiful as she is—is still growing in her understanding and confidence of who she needs to be. Yes, change has come slowly, but the generations are getting stronger. The revelation of God's plan and purpose on the earth is being brought to full bloom in even the hardest of hearts.

You can become for others what you did not have so that the generation following you will have your "faith stories" to lean on and your blessing to pass along.

In the *New Living Translation*, Psalm 78:7 says that "each generation should set its hope anew on God, not forgetting his glorious miracles and obeying his commands." Verse 8 goes on to say, "Then they will not be like their ancestors— stubborn, rebellious, and unfaithful, refusing to give their hearts to God."

These are such strategic days in which to live. And how we live is critical to the continued succession of what could be the greatest revolution of human hearts in history!

Coming to the forefront of this season in time is a great host of confident young men and women, people who were captivated at an early age by the awesome love of God and are seriously ready to lay down their lives for the sake of Christ. For you and me, that means growing pains as we now must lead this vast array of amazing people—older and younger, highly ambitious, extremely talented, opinionated, successful, and passionate. And, of course, there are also the undisciplined, some with less obvious talents, and scores of fatherless kids (often with no sense of boundary).

Personally, I have been forced to grow and stretch in my capacity to lead on every level. Many of the leadership themes we've taught our worship teams over the years have had little to do with musical understanding, but rather things like discipleship, self-worth, theology of worship, and God's unfailing love toward His people. And just as most great opportunities don't look like opportunities when they come to us as problems, I have honestly and continually had to ask God daily for His wisdom to lead well.

Wow, what a journey! What a God!

Mentoring: An Act of Obedience

Throughout the Psalms we find a consistent charge to earnestly take on the responsibility of declaring God's faithfulness to the next generation. We don't do so because we have a romantic notion about God or because we think that declaring His goodness is a nice idea—but because it's an act of obedience. King David understood this responsibility. In Psalm 71, we find David asking God to extend the breath of his life until he has adequately told the next generation of His greatness and power. Verse 18 says, "Yes, even when I am old and gray-headed, O God, forsake me not, [but keep me alive] until I have declared Your mighty

21

strength to [this] generation, and Your might and power to all that are to come" (AMP).

And in Psalm 145—one of my life's signature chapters that God uses frequently when speaking to me or challenging me—we find David again prophetically singing over the future generations, describing what you and I are a part of today and what has been gathering momentum for hundreds of years: The generations *are* being absolutely devoted and captivated by the glorious nature of our King.

Just as in David's day, there's much talk about mentoring the rising generations, and a lot of it sounds wonderful. However, the truth is that to foster the next generation, we must become selfless leaders who are not out to make a name or position for ourselves but rather willing to pass on our knowledge and understanding for the kingdom's sake. Like David, we must be ready to deny ourselves in order to protect those God has entrusted to us.

Second Samuel 23:15-17 tells of a time when David longed for a sip of water from the well of Bethlehem where he had often refreshed himself as a boy. When the three mighty men heard of his thirst, they broke through enemy lines, risking their lives, to fulfill his desire. True mentors win the hearts of those they lead. Therefore, the valiant warriors presented him with the water, thinking they were doing it for David. But David had his priorities in line with God's, and poured it out as a drink offering before the Lord. His life was not about meeting his own needs but about lifting up the name of the Lord no matter what the cost to himself.

When the Flesh Rules

It sounds easy, but church history proves that man has a tendency to put his own reputation and desire for recognition above all else. Too often, when those who follow us start to advance beyond what we have accomplished, jealousy prevails and the mentoring comes to a screeching halt. Then God must wait for another generation to be raised up, one with kingdom priorities.

True mentors win the hearts of those they lead.

In Deuteronomy 1 and 2, we read about the struggle Moses had with the double-minded Israelites who refused to believe God and make Him Lord of all, even though they were experiencing incredible favor and miraculous provision. Talk about a stubborn people! Under Moses' leadership, they were given a way out of the wilderness. God went before them, sending a fire by night and a cloud by day to show them the way. But they would not submit to God's plan or purpose for their lives. They thought they knew better than God, and that rebellious, disobedient attitude became their undoing.

The Lord himself finally told Moses in Deuteronomy 1:34–36, "No one from this evil generation shall see the good land I swore to give your ancestors, except Caleb son of Jephunneh. He will see it, and I will give him and his descendants the land he set his feet on, because he followed the Lord wholeheartedly." God had to wait thirty-eight years until that entire generation had passed away before His perfect will could be done on earth.

We parents know what it feels like to see our children make a willful decision to disobey. We struggle with disappointment in our kids and with doubts about our ability to handle the situation correctly.

We are racked with questions such as "Where have I gone wrong?" "Why isn't she listening?" "Why doesn't he see that the consequences of his choice will have a harsh outcome?"

I really do wonder at times how our God—who sees the end from the beginning and is all-knowing and all-powerful—must feel when we stray. How does He bear the pain of watching us make so many hasty, prideful, ignorant decisions that lack His understanding of the greater picture? Perhaps the answer lies in the example Moses provided. He is the real hero. As a leader, he just kept on keeping on, leading and directing those who would listen. He had learned that some will and some won't, but he would stay true to God. In Deuteronomy 4, Moses cautions, "The Lord your God destroyed from among you everyone who followed the Baal of Peor, but all of you who held fast to the Lord your God are still alive today. See, I have taught you decrees and laws as the Lord my God commanded me, so that you may follow them in the land you are entering to take possession of it. . . . Teach them to your children and to their children after them" (vv. 3–5, 9).

The Scriptures that follow provide some of the Bible's most powerful teaching on obedience and sacrifice—and then the Ten Commandments are laid out for all of us.

So why didn't Moses have more success in raising up that generation? Well, when we fail to successfully teach the principles of *why* we do certain things, the effectiveness of the outcome eventually wears down, and people begin to follow a system of routine to achieve results rather than living out of their convictions.

Some years ago, *Worth* magazine highlighted the problems associated with effectively communicating and teaching life principles. The article stressed the struggle of handing down generational wealth so that responsibility and understanding are also passed on. Needless to say, often when financial wealth is handed down to those who have not earned it themselves, those who receive it also lack the ability to manage it well.

The article noted, "By and large, inheritors of wealth have no appreciation of what is required to build it. The theory is that the first generation starts off in a rice paddy, meaning two people with an affinity for one another come together and create a financial fortune. The second generation moves to the city, puts on beautiful clothes, joins the opera board, runs big organizations, and the fortune plateaus. The third generation, with no experience of work, consumes the financial fortune, and the fourth generation goes back to the rice paddy."[1]

Know What You Teach, Teach What You Know

You might be thinking that the "rice paddy principle" really doesn't apply to you on either a financial or a spiritual level. However, when the *why* we do what we do doesn't permeate in *all* that we do, our value systems give evidence that we do not have enough truth to successfully support what we do and who we are. Our own lack of truth then becomes a stumbling block to sharing the knowledge, vision, and passions behind whatever it is we do and whoever it is we are. We cannot give away what we do not own, and that's why we need to have our own "faith stories" to pass on.

As spiritual moms and dads, we must be fully convinced of God's ability to work in our lives. Then we can lay hold of the wonderful privilege we have of passing down our knowledge, experience, example, and rich legacy of faith to the next generation, who will also need to remember that if God could do it then, He can do it now.

One problem we usually encounter is the lack of time needed to produce growth. Most of us are not very good at setting aside time to sit and converse at the levels needed to exchange truths. Or we are not very good at taking the time to listen to those who have been forging the path ahead of us. In both instances, without the appropriate teaching of a hands-on experience—and, may I say, without a personal revelation—it will be difficult to make stronger

Often when financial wealth is handed down to those who have not earned it themselves, those who receive it also lack the ability to manage it well.

25

what you have received from those who passed their inheritance on to you.

The church's history with regard to music is replete with historical examples of how one man failed to pass on his knowledge of music. Before the times of Handel and Bach, most church music was in the hands of laymen. Actually, in those days, the people known to have education and culture were those found in the church.

It was Saint Ambrose, Archbishop of Milan (from 374–397), who took a keen interest in music and introduced it to the church as prayers and worship. He devised a special form of chanting known as the Ambrosian chant. This caught on as a new song and echoed within the walls of many houses of worship. Sadly, however, when Ambrose died, church music in his sphere of influence died with him.

The Ambrosian chant was great for a season, but without generational revelation, "passing of the baton" never happened. It took another two hundred years before Pope Gregory introduced the house of God to a new method of song—the Gregorian chant was born. This time, due to its reason for existence and its methods of being taught to the younger generation, the chant is alive and well today.

Actually, if you ever have the opportunity to hear a Gregorian chant proclaimed in one of the grand cathedrals, don't judge it. Just close your eyes and think about the greatness of our God. Fix your thoughts on the sacrifices of those who have gone before you and allow your heart to be moved in a spectacular way. This experience always reminds me that someday my platform, that is, the platform of influence that God has given me, will actually become the starting point for someone else! It's a humbling thought.

And although I don't know what your platform of influence is, I do know that we all need a biblically rich understanding of *why* we do *what* we do—for we know that without vision, people perish. But guess what! With vision and understanding, they flourish! It's your vision and understanding that someone else needs for a starting point.

You and I must teach those we mentor that our lives are holy before God and that developing a lifestyle of worship is critical to maintaining the purity of our influence. Acts 10:15 (NKJV) warns us not to treat as common what God has cleansed.

This Scripture surely keeps bland living at a safe distance when you are a Christ follower. The problem is that we can easily become a bit familiar with either our current platform or the people around us, or even the presence of God. Familiarity can lead to apathy, and one morning we can wake up to find that we have lost our sense of awe for the things of God.

I like the way Matthew 7:6 reads in *The Message* translation: "Don't be flip with the sacred. Banter and silliness give no honor to God. Don't reduce holy mysteries to slogans. In trying to be relevant, you're only being cute and inviting sacrilege."

Give the Gift of Time

Now is the time, my friend, to pick up and dust off all the hopes and dreams that have been in your heart, even if you've had some disappointments along the way. Take a deep breath and simply get moving in your own lane, the one you know is waiting for you. Whether you are training others, or taking your first steps toward your heart's desires, take time for growth.

Young men and women with great skill, creativity, and passion surround us—people who need to hear our faith stories and have a safe place to grow up in. They need time with someone who will listen to their dreams and recognize their untapped potential. They need people like you and me to believe in them.

There is no substitute for time. Giving time is giving life to others. I've learned from my own children that quality time is quantity time and that to really hear their dreams and desires takes moments where I am not interrupted or distracted by anything else. In Philippians 2:4, Paul encouraged those who would follow his example: "Put yourself aside, and help others get ahead. Don't be obsessed with getting your own advantage. Forget yourselves long enough to lend a helping hand" (THE MESSAGE).

— Your life is all you have to give, so be generous with your time, especially toward those who are looking to you for leadership and wanting to follow your example.

— Let's be committed to growth, even though it mostly means change.

Honor all that has been, but lean into all that is to come. Together let's provide a good city to grow old in and a good city to grow up in.

"CHANGE IS INEVITABLE. GROWTH IS OPTIONAL."

John C. Maxwell

VALUE TWO:
ENCOURAGEMENT

*Let us consider how we may spur one another on . . . not giv-
ing up meeting together, as some are in the habit of doing, but
encouraging one another—and all the more as you see the Day
approaching.*

—Hebrews 10:24–25

Ignatius, who is said to have succeeded Peter as the ruling
elder of Antioch, had much to say about Hebrews 10:25,
including, "When ye frequently, and in numbers, meet
together, the powers of Satan are overthrown, and his
mischief is neutralized by your like-mindedness in the
faith." Simply put, we need each other. The devil is out
to dash our dreams and steal our hope for seeing God's
purposes fulfilled—not only in our own lives but also in the
lives of those we mentor. That's why God has summoned us
to stick together and to encourage one another in the faith.
It's in fellowship that our souls are mysteriously soothed, our
faith starts to soar, and our hearts are knit together in love.
There's nowhere on earth to find greater comfort, concern, and

connection than in God's family. But building relationships takes time, effort, and encouragement. And . . .

Time goes by so very fast.

I find it hard to fathom that my own firstborn daughter is now a married woman and mum to our first grandbaby, Ava Pearl. (What a gift to us all!) Sometimes a week can fly by so quickly that I'm often taken by surprise to find that Sunday has arrived again! And, with time fleeting so quickly, we must be continually aware of the urgency and value of preparing not only the next generation but also speaking life and potential into the third and fourth generations.

I will never forget when our dear friend Pastor Rick Godwin from San Antonio, Texas, said, "Darlene, the two greatest days of your life are the day you were born and the day you found out why." These words resonated so deeply within me that I can still recall clearly sensing that I had been "set apart" for kingdom endeavors. It's as if God flipped on the lights of my spirit so I could see where I was headed. God used Rick to drop an anchor in my heart that would keep me encouraged in the Lord. And history shows that all of the truly great men and women of God were, like Rick, committed to speaking encouragement, direction, and promise into the lives of others. Encouragement is a vital part of *who* we are as leaders and *what* we are to pour into the people we mentor.

I have many memories of my parents, grandparents, church leaders, and friends filling my soul with encouragement when I did not have the courage to believe in the dreams God had placed in my heart. Now, having visited churches throughout the globe, I have learned that many of the great men and women around us rarely receive the support needed to breathe life into their dreams. I find it so interesting that instead of lavishing encouragement on others, many leaders can be quite stingy in giving helpful words of encouragement to those around them. How can this be? If we are to follow the example of our God, encouragement ought to be our priority.

Psalm 10:16–18 says, "The Lord is King for ever and ever; the nations will perish from his land. You, Lord, hear the desire of the afflicted; you encourage them, and you listen to their cry, defending the fatherless and the oppressed so that mere earthly mortals will never again strike terror."

"The two greatest days of your life are the day you were born and the day you found out why."

You and I are on the earth as God's ambassadors to hear the desires of those whose goals have been afflicted. We are the ones called to alleviate their fears with the encouragement of our King.

Seeing What God Sees in People

There is a large publishing company in the United States that hired a human resource executive who was determined to encourage the staff. Alice was her name. And it was she who sent out an interoffice request asking employees to list some admirable qualities of co-workers in their department. The response was so positive that Alice had to pare down the lists. After many hours of preparation, each employee received a framed copy of the encouraging words their peers had used to describe them. You guessed it! The work atmosphere changed and people began to step out in confidence.

We all need people who will believe in us until we can believe in ourselves. Barnabas was that kind of support to the apostle Paul, overlooking his faults and lifting his reputation above his own. Later, however, when a young minister named John Mark failed to keep a commitment, Paul called him "unworthy" and wanted nothing to do with him. Barnabas and Paul were so polarized over Mark that they "separated from each other, and Barnabas took Mark with him and sailed away to Cyprus" (Acts 15:39 AMP). Barnabas went on to mentor Mark until Mark became such a dynamic force for the Lord that he wrote an entire book of the Bible. Imagine what you and I would have missed if Barnabas had not given Mark a chance to recover from his failure. As leaders, we need to be more like Barnabas, encouraging those who have failed and showing them how to get up so they can live the life they were intended to live. We need to look beyond faults and magnify the possibilities in those we mentor, refusing to give up on them until they believe in themselves.

─ As people mature, they learn to encourage themselves in the Lord, just as King David did. We can find ourselves being genuinely encouraged from something we've read, heard, seen, or experienced that becomes a kiss from heaven to warm our hearts and remind us that God is with us. For example, I am encouraged when I listen to good music, or see an amazing garden, or gaze upon a lovely piece of art. I am encouraged when I hear someone preaching a great message, and when I see my family doing life well and working harmoniously together. I am encouraged when I see my husband reading and studying the Word, or when I read about someone who, against all odds, has achieved success.

Yes, life presents many, many moments—if we choose to look for them—that have the power to strengthen our hope in the Lord.

Fueling Hope and Confidence

What is it that encourages you?

I recently asked a close girlfriend that question when she was feeling low, and she could not find her answer. But she has one—we all do. We simply need to ask the right questions to draw out of another those things that have become buried in the heart. Then the answers will come. When you know how to encourage yourself in the Lord, you'll be able to use your experiences to help others when they are feeling defeated and needing a reason to keep going.

For some reason, I was able at an early age to tap into music's capacity to soothe and encourage my soul. It lifts me emotionally and comforts me when no one is there to hear my heart. I've learned to fill my life with worshipful music, and again and again I see music do what it was created to do—fill the atmosphere with the presence of the Lord.

The language of music has always fascinated me because it gives voice to the human journey and becomes a vehicle of expression that is far deeper than words alone can ever convey. Music communicates our cries, our anguish, our joy—the highs and lows of life. David says in Psalm 71:23, "When I open up in song to you, I let out lungsful of praise, my rescued life a song" (THE MESSAGE). I wish I could tell you how much I love that verse.

As a young woman struggling to find the length and breadth of God's ministry plans for my life, some people would try to bring me back to earth, so to speak, when I shared the purposes and intents of my heart. I was young and full of enthusiasm, full of passion for music, and hungry for knowledge about worship. But when I shared the vastness of my ministry goals, others often tried to dissuade me, saying they did not want me to be disappointed.

For years I wondered why people felt the need to "small me down." That's not the way God sees us. In Psalm 139:17, we read, "How precious are your thoughts about me, O God. They cannot be numbered!" Verse 18 goes on to say, "I can't even count them; they outnumber the grains of sand! And when I wake up, you are still with me" (NLT).

All Different but Equally Valued

As I've traveled the world, rather than finding that the multitudes are thinking more highly of themselves than they ought, I have honestly found that most Christians think too lowly of themselves. But it doesn't take much of a language shift to ensure that what we bring to others is the power of acceptance and support.

I have never seen a more simple strategy have such a brilliant impact!

Every single person needs to know he or she is valued and completely valuable.

However, even when we're told we are valued, it's often difficult to realize that God's desire to bless us will always exceed our ability to receive. I remember when my pastor asked me to take on the worship department of our church. The Holy Spirit wrote Psalm 45 across the fabric of my being for three whole days and nights. Finally, we took our little family off to the beach for a mini holiday to talk and pray about the ramifications of our decision. I was simply overwhelmed. My mind was bombarded with fearful thoughts and feelings of inadequacy. What if I failed and took the whole worship department down with me! Thankfully, God didn't leave me there. As I stood at the edge of the ocean early one morning, I sensed Him saying that I could choose, and whichever way I went, He would give me wisdom, moment by moment, and grace for each day.

I kept thinking about a verse I read near the end of Psalm 45: "Your sons will take the place of your fathers; you will make them princes throughout the land" (v. 16).

At the time, it made no sense to me. But now as the years have evolved and my heart has become more refined and secure with the message of releasing others—well, now it definitely makes sense. God has revealed again and again His heart for succession and multiplication, releasing the sons and the daughters. So this Scripture points to the time when generational transition happens well, releasing the children to greater heights upon which to reign in life. Completely stunning!

God created man and woman to be sons and daughters, humankind (or kind humans), different but equal, to have dominion, made in His image. Oh, and what a great idea! And how wonderful it is to see the sons and daughters reigning well together.

It's often difficult to realize that God's desire to bless us will always exceed our ability to receive.

I have friends who work tirelessly throughout India—feeding, teaching, and believing in a seemingly forgotten generation. What a privilege it is to watch their strategy with those young women who have been denied the right to an education (let's change this!). They have used the encouragement strategy to transform an atmosphere of hopelessness into one of grand possibility, time and time again. They fill the atmosphere with praise and life and genuine encouragement, and then watch God do the miraculous. Where possibility is allowed to reign, life breeds greater life. An outstanding God principle!

You Can Do It!

You may not know right now who to pour your life into, but I would suggest that you start with the first one God brings your way, younger or older. What could be more gratifying than to discover someone's potential and then become the one who helps to develop it? When your words have caused someone to rise out of the ashes and know that they are loved, appreciated, and have a future worth showing up for—you have made headline news in heaven!

And speaking of news, in many places there is a language shift from a prevailing language of negativity to a culture of hard work and possibility, where you can sense an atmosphere of "Whatever it takes, we will do it!" It's a charge made famous by Mother

Teresa, who was renowned for taking whatever was in her hand and turning it into whatever the need required.

I would like to take this idea a step further and put it in a "releasing others" framework, such as, "Hey, whatever it takes— *you* can do it!" Not out of "passing the buck," but because none of us can do everything. We need each other's gifts, talents, and skills to do the work of the Lord. Empowering others is the key here. This is the beauty of the body: We all have something to contribute; therefore, we need to discover what that is and believe that we can do it. Then it's our job to find out what others have and release them into the life they were intended to live, even if it far exceeds our own.

When you start to share the workload and the responsibility and the credit, you light a fire deep inside of others, giving them the experience and helping them to work out that which is buried within. Encouragement is a powerful force, and when it is given sincerely and often, the creative dynamic over a lifetime has the ability to see the seemingly ordinary rise to become exceedingly abundantly above and beyond anything that could have been hoped for or imagined. God's plans for us are huge, and when we walk in them, we glorify Him.

———

The group Delirious wrote a song, "Our God Reigns," that has a powerful lyric: "He's a Father who loves to parade you"—it gets me every time.[1]

Imagine that!

The God who created the heavens and the earth actually enjoys showing off His children—you and me!

God's heart is always for us, and yet I have seen too many Christians living with a crippled sense of self-worth. We all have our "brain battles" with Satan, the accuser of the brethren, who lies to our minds about who we are and what we can do. However, when we start to agree with his lies about us, our passion for life and the possibilities that it holds dwindles and we can become bound in anger and resentment. All too often, people who feel minimized, disregarded, or unworthy will live below their God-given potential merely to fit in or be accepted. We all need encouragement.

My prayer is that we leaders would cultivate an unselfish, unspoiled, and generous-hearted love.

The grossly misled worth systems of our world can easily stuff the wrong values down our throats. If you are not wealthy, or well-known . . . if you're not thin enough, accepted enough, or even normal enough . . . if your friends are not part of the in crowd, etc., then the courageous person you know yourself to be on the inside feels so inferior that it seems easier to stay small than to resist the tide of our culture. And when those in your immediate surroundings are saying, "You'll never amount to anything; who do you think you are?" . . . well, you have one daunting obstacle to overcome. But hey, whatever it takes—you can do it!

Words to Blanket Our Hearts

Words carry life.

Proverbs 15:4 says, "The soothing tongue is a tree of life, but a perverse tongue crushes the spirit." When someone's spirit is crushed by criticism and abuse, his or her emotional energy is zapped, and more energy is required to see potential released. But when the words coming from you are filled with support, the tree of life brings forth beautiful fruit.

I personally lived most of my childhood so internally tormented with insecurity that its effects caused my body to shut down. I became bulimic, and the nature of that lifestyle troubled my spirit until my own naturally happy heart was overwhelmed.

I grew up singing, being encouraged by a mum who thought

the sun shone out from me (she still does, that's a mother's love!), but despite all that support, the enemy would still try to tear my soul apart. Aside from my own family, who did their best to console me, God used two women in my local church, Beth and Desley, who literally came alongside me, accepted me, encouraged me, welcomed me into their homes, and just happened to be the leaders of the music department (how lovely is God to set that up!). Beth and Desley loved me amidst all my tenderhearted but very misguided baggage.

I am forever grateful to them for loving and inspiring me as they did—cheering me on in my dreams, encouraging me in my giftings, and, even more important, showing me the way to God.

Of course, the enemy of our souls recognizes our potential too. What I see in the Bible is that children and infants filled with God-designed purpose and potential have always been targeted by the enemy in order to cut short their destiny before they learn for themselves that the name of Jesus is greater than any trial. Psalm 8 declares the power released from the mouths and hearts of praising children as they indeed silence the enemy with their stance of faith.

The problems come when we place our faith in man rather than God. Years ago now, one of our young worship leaders was supposed to be leading a service but was nowhere to be found. I knew I had seen his car so I went outside to look for him. Sensing something was amiss, I followed my instinct, and sure enough, there he was, sitting in the gutter on the side of the parking lot, just staring into space. After some casual chatting, he opened up to me and confessed that he just didn't have what it takes to be a leader.

During that season, a few well-known ministers around the world had made foolish choices, and as a young man of God, his faith in himself was shaken when his mentors fell. I felt so sad for him and wished I could gather the pieces of his broken heart and instantly put them all back together. I couldn't. But what I did discover that day was the power of encouraging words to help him get back on his feet. He's now one of the finest worship leaders and writers I know—generous to the core, and so tenderhearted toward broken humanity that his life is a great inspiration to Mark and me and countless others.

Encouraging words, fueled by the Word of God, carry life. They are like a cold drink of the finest water to a desperately thirsty soul. Even the smallest act of kindness can bring hope to a hurting heart.

I've seen the words "That was wonderful! Well done!" breathe a quiet assurance into the heart of someone who was insecure about preaching, leading, playing. When training up new leaders of worship—or if there is a leader feeling particularly vulnerable at a certain time—one simple thing I do is to stand where I can be seen from the corner of their eye, to simply cheer them on with a nod, or an expression of approval. I like to act as an inconspicuous security blanket for those who need some extra encouragement. It's one way of simply setting others up to win.

It's so important to help others see that an error does not create a blemish on their character. I so believe in talking through the mistakes and helping those we are leading to see that these are opportunities for learning. We need to fail forward together.

It is a very insecure, manipulative leader who will take someone's character to task over a simple, innocent mistake.

Throughout the years, I've seen hundreds of men and women leave churches or ministry because mistakes were not handled compassionately and were not confronted in love. Instead, the people in the hot seat either were not addressed and never used again or were berated publicly only to be lost in a sea of humiliation. Much of what we do in music ministry happens in a public arena, so there is less room for error and certainly nowhere to hide when you make a blunder.

41

It is a very insecure, manipulative leader who will take someone's character to task over a simple, innocent mistake.

Let's remember that everyone fails, we just fail differently. And everyone needs encouragement, but it is critical to those in the early stages of development and to those who have made an error and now feel emotionally fragile.

I have personally made my share of mistakes while leading worship, speaking, and just doing life. That's when humor comes in handy; it buffers the pain. We all need to cultivate the ability to laugh at ourselves and treat ourselves with kindness when we've made an innocent mistake.

Kindness is infectious—so is generosity. It stirs greatness in the spiritual realm and changes both the giver and the receiver.

I was recently admiring a young musician's expensive new guitar and noticed that he was treating it like a firstborn child. I commented, "You must have worked and saved a long time for it." With tears in his eyes, he explained that a guy on the team had given him the guitar to encourage his desire to play and write songs. It was a costly act of generosity and encouragement that will leave a lasting legacy.

I too have experienced that kind of generosity and encouragement. Years ago, a dear friend was simply praying about God's will for her life when she received an instruction from heaven. She called to say she had a gift for me and wanted me to receive it ASAP! I was intrigued and excited. However, I was absolutely astonished when she said she needed to give me her grand piano. What she didn't know is that I had been praying for a piano to use for creating music and worshiping the Lord. (I had not asked for a grand, and am still very humbled by her act of generosity.)

I so did not expect such an extravagant gift, but wow, the encouragement I received that day—it still makes my heart smile.

That piano sits in the middle of our lounge room. It's in the heart of our home, and each time I see it, play it, or hear my children playing it, I am inspired to praise the God of heaven and earth for hearing my prayers and hearing the prayers of my friend. We were both blessed and honored by the outcome. You see, encouragement is active, not passive, and so illuminating for both the giver and the receiver.

I like the way 1 Corinthians 8:1 says it: "[Yet mere] knowledge causes people to be puffed up (to bear themselves loftily and be proud), but love (affection and goodwill and benevolence) edifies and builds up and encourages one to grow [to his full stature]" (AMP).

A Heart for People

One of the most encouraging leaders I have ever met is Pastor Tommy Barnett from Phoenix First Assembly of God. He is a church pastor, church planter, and founder of the Dream Center. His church is known as "The church with a heart," and its reputation is well earned. Pastor Tommy often says, "Find a need and fill it; find a hurt and heal it." He has personally encouraged me many times, and when Mark and I first embarked on a new season of ministry together as senior pastors of Hope Unlimited Church on the coast north of Sydney, it was his encouragement that gave us the strength to soar.

I've heard Joyce Meyer say that, apart from her husband, the one extra person she would love to take on all her trips is Pastor Tommy, because of his ability to encourage. He has stood in many a meeting where I have led worship and come up afterward to pour words of life over me. When he's around, you feel like you can do anything! And the amazing thing is, he lives like that every day . . . with every person he meets—his children, his staff, those he personally leads, and those he mentors. Pastor Tommy does not reserve his encouraging words for Sundays, or for those who could reciprocate with favors. No, this man's life is the epitome of encouragement. I once asked him a few questions about raising up another generation and here's that dialogue:

What would you say was your greatest joy in ministry?
Seeing my children serving God and all three working with me in the ministry!

What is your biggest frustration when training younger ministers?
Watching them wanting it all now! Not enjoying the "journey."

What is the one thing you would want a younger pastor/leader to take into his future in serving God?
Know that living a righteous life is the number one priority, because righteousness and provision for the vision go together: "Seek first the kingdom of God and all these other things will be added."

In your opinion, what would be the main obstacle that takes young men and women out of the ministry?
Discouragement! And they give up too quickly!

With your own children, what has been the most important value you have shown them about serving God and all that this means?
Keep your eyes on God and then the God-given vision for your life. Men at best are just men. But God never fails!!!

Thanks, Pastor Tommy.

———

When there has been a huge lack of encouraging words spoken over you, you need to learn how to build yourself up with the Word of God. Don't wait for everyone else to lift your spirits. Even if you are in a tough or dry season, stir yourself up. Position words of life wherever you spend time so that even if you don't feel like getting happy, you cannot avoid it.

When my dear girlfriend lost her first child, she surrounded herself with promises from Scripture and played loud worship music until the neighbors almost moved out! She didn't feel like reading words of life, but she did it anyway. We all watched as the Master Shepherd personally tended oh so carefully to the heart of this great woman . . . and she has emerged with grace and dignity, just as the Bible declares.

Encouragement, the Cure for *Idle*

On one of my husband's first trips into East Africa, Mark met with lots of pastors and leaders from different denominations and many of the local government representatives. They discussed ways we Westerners could be a benefit to their land and how we could best serve the people. The ideas for both immediate and long-term help were great. Mark was fueled by the grassroots, real conversations he had had about stretching the available resources in order to make the greatest impact.

However, the one question he was unprepared for came from a youth leader.

"Can you teach us how to think?"

Mark was floored. This young minister went on to explain that even if millions of dollars were poured into the land that very day, they lacked the correct procedure, energy, and creative wisdom needed to facilitate that kind of gift. Creativity was not encouraged or found among the youth who would become the leaders of tomorrow. Actually, what we discovered in many of these developing nations is something known as *idle*, a greater epidemic than HIV/AIDS or malaria.

It's easy to see how people slip into a state of being idle. The unemployment rate is high, there's a lack of education and

45

opportunity, no one to encourage their dreams, and no funds available to support any ambition. There's simply nowhere to go and nothing to do. *Idle* means you don't dream, because you don't want to be disappointed.

People all over the world are living in varied states of war, poverty, disease, hunger, and ruin. The fact that they still get up in the morning is a miracle to me. Ahhh, but such is the resilience of the human spirit. For when God made us, He created a one-of-a-kind masterpiece with a will to live and a purpose to fulfill. With just a little encouragement, anyone can change. Some of the great initiatives being implemented in the developing world are ingenious. Young people don't really want a handout; they want something that gives them dignity, and it starts with encouragement.

Everyone—whether young or old, rich or poor, black or white—needs encouragement. If you are being mentored right now, please be an encourager to those who are leading you. When I was in the stretch, someone from the team would usually write me a note, come alongside, or bring a meal to let me know that I was loved and appreciated—expressions of encouragement that kept me steadfast when I wanted to run away.

Your encouragement could be the fuel that someone desperately needs to finish the race. Job 4:4 says, "Your words have held firm him who was falling, and you have strengthened the feeble knees" (AMP). With encouragement, the powers of Satan are overthrown, and we can live the life of purpose that God intends for us to live.

"WHEN SOMEONE
ENCOURAGES
YOU,
THAT PERSON HELPS YOU OVER
A THRESHOLD
YOU MIGHT OTHERWISE
NEVER HAVE CROSSED
ON YOUR
OWN."[2]

John O'Donohue

VALUE THREE:
20/20 DREAMS AND VISIONS

And then God answered: "Write this. Write what you see. Write it out in big block letters so that it can be read on the run. This vision-message is a witness pointing to what's coming. It aches for the coming—it can hardly wait! And it doesn't lie. If it seems slow in coming, wait. It's on its way. It will come right on time."
—Habakkuk 2:2–3
The Message

The aging medical missionary Albert Schweitzer was asked, "How goes it with you, Dr. Schweitzer?" With all the enthusiasm of a young man, he responded, "My eyesight grows dim, but my vision is clearer than ever."

I am grateful to have always been part of a church that is full of vision, vision that is constantly growing clearer than ever. Even in my first church, where I was saved at fifteen, something was always going on to help build the lives of others.

During our time at Hillsong, my family and I have been privileged to be under a spiritual covering that is not afraid to dream God-sized dreams. And as we've sat under Pastor Brian Houston's leadership these many years, he has often said that we will always have way more vision than money—the God gap is always there! And that's a good thing! The God gap keeps us dependent on His ability to do the impossible while we are hard at work doing the possible. The great thing about sharing in a God-sized dream is that you get to partner with God to build the lives of others.

Expand Your Vision

Not long after giving birth to our third daughter, Zoe Jewel, I was sitting in the kitchen holding the baby and watching our two other little girls at play outside, when I turned to my husband and said with a contented sigh, "I feel like I am living my dream." Mark quickly but lovingly replied, "Well, it's time to start dreaming bigger!"

Stunned, I had to take a deep breath and let his words sink in before I realized what he meant: If you stop dreaming, you get complacent, and complacency never changes the world.

On our wedding day, Mark and I committed our lives to serving and honoring God with *all* that we have and *all* that we are. Instinctively, we both knew that every vision would require inspiration, perspiration, and passion. To find energy and passion for birthing what's in my heart, I only have to reflect on Calvary and all that Jesus has done for us. This realization makes me want to squeeze every drop out of each opportunity we have to share Christ, and to use all our gifts and talents to make Him known to the rising generations and to the unreached people groups in the world.

We will always have way more vision than money—the God gap is always there!

In Matthew 28:19, Jesus shared His vision for those of us who believe in Him: "Go and make disciples of all nations." What this looks like will be different for each one of us, but Acts 17:28 tells us how it is possible: "In him we live and move and have our being." God himself is there to make His heart known to us, to love us, and to bring to fruition the dreams and visions He has placed in our hearts. But if we inadvertently preach a modern-day Christianity of mediocrity, or fail to let others consider the cost, or share a message of convenience when we share Christ, we fall into the trap of presenting a lifestyle choice rather than the choice to lay down our lives and follow Him.

When I said yes to Jesus, I said yes to all that following Him means. I said yes to Someone to live for and Someone to die for—a message of great grace, of great surrender, of forgiveness and healing, and of the greatest love ever known.

Out of the revelation of being loved came *vision*. His love for me opened the eyes of my heart and I found the hope and freedom to trust God for everything. With His vision of me came a gift of confidence that I could never have imagined before my Jesus-encounter.

So for those of you lacking in sparkle for the future, whether young or old, in transition or not, it's time to start dreaming bigger and asking God to put dreams in your heart that are worthy of His great love for you. It's time to talk about the impossible coming to pass and taking the blinders off the eyes of your heart so you can get brave with vision.

I have always loved this Scripture about faith: "Now faith is the substance of things hoped for, the evidence of things not seen" (Hebrews 11:1 NKJV).

You cannot see faith, but you can hang your life on it. It's evident even though you can't see it.

Vision has similar attributes, which is why Habakkuk tells us to write the vision down and make it plain, that those who see it may run with it.

As Mark and I have run our race, we have endeavored not only to speak about what we see in our future but also to write it down, read it, and measure our pace with it. This discipline keeps us accountable, especially when life has thrown a curve ball and times are tough. It's during those times that the written vision shines like a torch, reminding us of the possibilities that lie before us. As leaders, we also have a responsibility to teach others how to find their dreams and follow them.

Stepping Into the God Gap

Many years ago I asked our team, "What would you do with your life if there were no limits, no financial barriers, nothing in the way to hold you back?"

The answers were interesting, and it became obvious to me that some of the team had given this subject a great deal of thought. The majority, however, had simply settled for very feasible outcomes. Their answers could quite easily have been achieved with careful planning, some tenacity, and a bit of good business sense. I went home that night feeling quite burdened to pray, "God, how on earth do we encourage people to dream bigger, to think outside the box, to actually speak out and go for some of the desires that you have placed in their hearts?"

I've come to realize that most people don't understand the "God gap." They think the outcome relies on their own ability, and unachieved dreams and visions will reflect poorly on their faith or reputation. And I also understand that some people struggle with a lack of confidence, or a fear of what others will think, or a fear of failure. They compare themselves with others and see themselves as inferior—so they refuse to take risks.

But as a leader today, and as one who is still discovering all that is in my own heart, I encourage you to be brave and write down some of your own unuttered dreams and passions—no matter how impossible they might seem. Don't look back on past failures or shortcomings, but trust God to give you a *now* vision. As Mother Teresa once said, "Yesterday is gone. Tomorrow has not yet come. We have only today. Let us begin."

It's hard to find your spiritual eyesight when you are weary, downcast, or physically tired. So be sure to get some rest, tend to your soul, and strengthen your inner man.

For me, that means sitting at my piano and worshiping the Lord, or opening my Bible and simply meditating on the Word. You may want to go for a walk and just talk to God, or find a quiet place to pick up your journal and start releasing your feelings on paper.

Look up! There's more vision in you than you think!

One of the hardest things to find is time: time to listen, to think, and to consider the stirrings in your heart. As busy as life may be, take time, as precious as it is, to feed your soul and simply hear the voice of God tending to your inner man.

Billy Graham set a wonderful example. Early in life he wrote a personal vision statement: "My one purpose in life is to help people find a personal relationship with God, which I believe comes through knowing Christ." That statement governed his choices, his studies, and his priorities throughout his entire life.

Live Your Life Dreaming

You don't have to worry about getting it wrong or missing the mark. Take heart with this word from Proverbs 16:9: "In their hearts humans plan their course, but the Lord establishes their steps." Did you hear that? God will steer you in the right direction.

Maybe you've made some wrong turns in the past. Well, when you fill your heart and mind with a new vision, you won't have time to worry about regrets. Philippians 3:13 says that we are to keep "forgetting those things which are behind and reaching forward to those things which are ahead" (NKJV). Let go of those historical thoughts. Don't let the hurts, disappointments, and regrets of the past cripple your present or define your future.

Forgive.

You can have an incredible vision, but if your heart is tangled up in unforgiveness, you are not free to pursue it. If you are a leader who is heavy laden with disillusionment, your sphere of influence will suffer until you let it go. So do whatever is necessary to break off those things that are besetting you. Ask for forgiveness, seek some good counsel, or get alone with your heavenly Father and ask Him to heal the brokenness in your heart. God is faithful. When your heart is unencumbered, your dreams and visions will surface.

It's exciting to see those things that start as a simple thought—a momentary, fleeting thought—actually come to life. That's often how songs are birthed. I have ideas for songs, melodies, sounds, chords, and lyrics all floating around in my heart and head, a scary place to live at times—one foot in heaven and the other on earth, absolutely no use to anyone. Ahhh!

That's how it is.

But hours or weeks or months later, I'll be singing that song to a congregation and—even more astonishing—they'll be singing it with me. I think about the power of bringing to the fore that which is in your heart. And it doesn't go from your heart to your hand by wishing it there. It comes by sticking to it, working diligently, listening and learning, and living with the conviction that the Spirit of the Lord is upon my life with purpose. God is always multiplying and adding to our dreams, and the purpose is more clearly unveiled as you and I pursue the process.

For example, the journey Mark and I and our family are now on at Hope Unlimited Church started as a tender thought that maybe we could pioneer again . . . get involved in a flourishing community that was desperate for a church family—and so we just started bathing that thought in prayer. We also started having healthy conversations with good friends about the possibilities, and even went to spy out the land—and the more Mark spoke about it, the clearer the vision became. As time passed, the way forward became stronger and stronger until the vision is so alive in us now that our hearts have become brave enough to step into what we believe is God's plan for this time in our lives. But without the dream, and without the process we went through to gain a clear vision, I doubt we would have attempted the initial steps toward taking this new ground.

Leaders, live your life dreaming! Dreamers who can communicate their heart are so inspiring to be around. And let those you mentor dream too!

Don't be threatened! God is not limited. He has something for you that will perfectly fit your gifts, talents, and calling. As you embrace your vision with passion for God and trust in His ability to do the impossible, the ones you mentor will embrace it too. Write it, talk it, anchor it in your heart—let those who run with you carry it too. God delights in seeing dreams that are able to transition from one generation to the next.

King David put God at the center of all that he did. He had a vision for building a temple that would glorify God—a temple that would far exceed his own palace. He gathered the materials to build the temple and then allowed Solomon to complete the dream. Big dreamers produce dream builders!

We have always encouraged our children to dream big. And they do! Our middle daughter, Chloe, is studying architecture. She has incredible focus, and dreams of designing and building sustainable, state-of-the-art housing for the developing world. She *When your heart is unencumbered, your dreams and visions will surface.*

is such an amazing girl, and Mark and I marvel at the way she will have an idea in her mind and then think, dream, take time to let the thoughts simmer—and before long, the pencil is on the paper writing the vision that she saw with the eyes of her heart. As she starts to run with the vision, it takes on dimension and special definition until it finally becomes a reality.

What could you see for your life if it had no limitations? Don't be afraid to dream beyond your own capabilities. Who says you can't do all that is in your heart to do! Remember, we do the possible and God does the impossible. If it's a God-sized dream, it will take God's part to fill it—the God gap is always there. But His ways are not our ways, and He does not operate by the world's standards or economies.

Big dreamers produce dream builders!

His heart is *for* you . . . but you have to take the first step. Make the choice to live with purpose and do the next thing He puts in your heart to do. Inactivity is the thief of our times, but activity with no purpose is also a thief—so grab hold of God's vision for you.

Write it down, make it plain . . . dream big . . . go crazy!

"I WOULD GIVE ALL THE WEALTH OF THE WORLD, AND ALL THE DEEDS OF ALL THE HEROES, FOR ONE TRUE VISION."[1]

Henry David Thoreau

VALUE **FOUR:**
ENERGY

What I'm getting at, friends, is that you should simply keep on doing what you've done from the beginning. When I was living among you, you lived in responsive obedience. Now that I'm separated from you, keep it up. Better yet, redouble your efforts. Be energetic in your life of salvation, reverent and sensitive before God. That energy is God's energy, an energy deep within you, God himself willing and working at what will give him the most pleasure.

—Philippians 2:12
THE MESSAGE

On a dark, cloudy day in 1752, Benjamin Franklin decided to fly a kite and prove to the world that lightning, which he called liquid fire, could be channeled and controlled to produce electricity. With the help of his son, William, Ben tied a key to the end of the silk ribbon that held their kite and then set the kite aloft, sailing it directly into a rain cloud. When lightning struck the kite, its energy traveled down the ribbon and hit the key, producing sparks that sent a shock through Ben's knuckles. He suddenly realized that lightning's energy not only produces electricity but it also passes from one body to another. The great inventor's discovery altered forever the way the world would receive light, communication, and connection.

You might think it unusual to call energy a value; yet, like lightning, it is one of those "indefinables" that we all need in order to bring light, communication, and connection to others. We are the keys that spark life into idle hearts and hands. We also carry the Holy Spirit's energy and power. John 10:10 says we are to have life "in abundance (to the full, till it overflows)" (AMP). That sounds like energy to me!

In leadership, energy is one of the essential ingredients needed for bringing any sense of *new* to the table. It's energy that produces excitement in others.

You can either feed or starve your energy levels, depending on what you hear, what you read, the conversations you engage in, who you keep company with, and the thoughts you choose to dwell on. Yes, everything can affect your energy levels, and I have found that when leading others, great energy is expended and expected.

The Israelites—who were so long in the wilderness—had to *daily* gather up fresh manna, food from heaven, to sustain their lives. There was no such thing as heavenly leftovers! And their story reveals a God principle for all of us too. We need to be daily energized and fueled by God himself. We need to be inspired with His answers and His supply every single day. We do this by reading the Word of God—I mean really reading it, and welcoming its power in our lives. His Word then becomes the "liquid fire" flowing through us that sparks a desire to worship Him, lifting our voices, our prayers, and our praise to Him. And it's His power flowing through us that ultimately fulfills us as we serve.

I have found that when leading others, great energy is expended and expected.

Energy for the Journey

One of the things that energizes my husband, Mark, is collecting and reading old and rare books written to record the lives of great men and women who've gone before us. These books are filled with miracle stories that demonstrate the unrelenting faithfulness of God. They recount times of incredible revival, telling story after story of how God moved into a village and brought salvation and social reform.

I, too, have an insatiable appetite for these books. The stories are jaw-dropping and the inspiration is endless! Often, at the front of these books is a handwritten note of encouragement from one disciple to another for his or her journey of faith.

One book, entitled *Men of Fire*, written by Walter Russell Bowie (1961), says right at the top, "To the men of Virginia Seminary who for many generations have carried the gospel fire." This inscription intrigued me and caused me to spend time researching this author's life. I wanted to find out about his salvation experience and his passion for Christ, to learn about the fire of God in him and how it caused him to live a life that made such a difference.

I uncovered a man who had energy for relationships, study, marriage, and taking the gospel to as many people as possible during his lifetime. His biography reveals that he was a priest, author, educator, hymn writer, and lecturer in the Episcopal Church.

Bowie was ordained as a priest in 1909, serving at three Episcopalian churches and two theological seminaries. He served as a Red Cross chaplain at Base Hospital 45 in France during World War I. And he was greatly known for standing up for the impoverished and making a difference in the Social Gospel, which gained great momentum through his life of faith and works. In the book, he writes about the fire of conviction, the fire of the Holy Spirit, this unrelenting life-force at work in him, producing an energy that could not be explained away.

I love that he penned a book that would stir his own spirit and the spirit of many others, including myself, with numerous stories of men who had a conversion experience that could not be denied. One of the great by-products of this "new life" experience was energy for the journey. Over and over the story is told that when you have not only vision and focus but also Holy Spirit fire alive in you, energy comes.

Isaiah 40:31 tells us how to find energy for the journey: "But those who hope in the Lord will renew their strength. They will soar on wings like eagles; they will run and not grow weary, they will walk and not be faint."

You Are God's Lightning Rod

And talk about putting your hope in the Lord! We once had the privilege of holding a worship conference in Toulon, France, where we were hosted by an amazing group of nuns and volunteers from Europe. These women were generous to the core—their service humbling us in a way that I pray will always impact my life. Many of the people present that day were so enthusiastic in their faith that they wanted to keep on talking to us about the fire that burned in their bellies for the things of God. They hungered for more of what only God had in store—devoted Christ followers who had given up their jobs and were living by faith to travel wherever they could to share their faith and hope in the Lord. I heard the word *salvation* time and time again as young men and women poured out the contents of their hearts to me and the team, aching for God to move in their cities.

Wow, I just want to get up and declare over nations Chris Tomlin's song "God of This City"[1]—Bring it on!

Of course, the fire I'm referring to is what generations have used as a term to describe the Holy Spirit. In reading about the saints of old and hearing the testimonies of today's saints, and even speaking from our own personal experience, there's a power available to us through the third person of the Trinity, the Holy Spirit, that cannot be explained away, no matter how hard some may try.

In Acts 1:8, the Word clearly explains, "You will receive power when the Holy Spirit comes on you; and you will be [His] witnesses . . . to the ends of the earth." Again, the energy and life available to see His will done on earth through us is very real and very attainable.

Romans 15:13 says, "May the God of hope fill you with all joy and peace as you trust in him, so that you may overflow with hope by the power of the Holy Spirit."

Here's some great news: "Not by might nor by power, but by my Spirit. . . ." What this passage from Zechariah 4:6 means to you and those you mentor is that you don't have to be an extrovert or have a sanguine personality to lead or follow with energy. You are a lightning rod to carry the energy that hope creates by the Spirit of God. And when the bedrock of all you're living for is Christ and His kingdom, there's no life-sustaining force like it.

One of my dear friends who had been dealing with some depression found that she had no energy for anything, which was really out of character for her. As we talked about the fact that all her kids were growing up and leaving home, we tapped into the root of the matter. Life had changed for her and would never be as it was with little ones running about her feet, looking to her as their superstar.

It's tough to let go.

Anyway, I asked a few questions to draw out what was in her heart: "What would you be doing if you could do absolutely anything? What do you love to do? What is your key passion or gift?" At first, there was a stunned silence. Then she burst into tears, crying and crying, as she realized that now because her kids didn't need her every day, she didn't feel like she had much to contribute to church or society. And that feeling of uselessness opened the door for depression to keep her in the grip of its nasty claws. But my friend is a champion! An overcomer! And one day she finally had a revelation from the Lord that as long as she stayed down on herself, she would never have the energy to get up and help others.

After pondering the things that formerly brought her joy, she determined that her passion was helping, serving, and fostering other families. So bit-by-bit, she did her homework, found out about needs she could meet in her local area, and WOW! This girl has really come alive!

Now that is energizing!

Sow Energy, Reap Energy

Years ago, at one of our church staff meetings, Pastor Jonathan Wilson, who now pastors Newport Church in California, spoke about energy, and said: "If you want to reap energy, you have to sow energy."

Simple yet profound!

And that principle works in every facet of life, especially the physical. After my fortieth birthday, I seriously had to increase my exercise routine and start running to maintain my natural energy levels.

We reap what we sow.

Likewise, the older I get and the more church services and meetings I am a part of, the more I need to be found in the Word, embracing God's pattern and teaching. It's not simply about hearing more messages, but digging into the Word for myself and allowing my hunger for His presence to be evident and worked out through my life as His Spirit sustains and inspires me.

If you wonder how on earth you're going to find it in yourself to lift again, to bring an energy that you feel isn't even there for this next season, then it's time to start sowing energy!

As long as she stayed down on herself, she would never have the energy to get up and help others.

Much of life is so daily and so routine that we can get bogged down with the monotony of it. If you're a mother, that's especially true—getting dressed and fed, dressing and feeding and prepping all the others, making beds, doing laundry, attending meetings, cooking, shopping, teaching, homework, rehearsals. Ahhh, the glamour life!

But when you walk out your days with *God's intent* at the core of all that you do, a renewed energy is found.

As leaders, we must display consistencies that are tried and true and are nonnegotiable—and leaning into Holy Spirit-infused energy is one of them. It's especially frustrating to be around leaders who are initially so energized for an idea that everyone gets behind it, but then the idea wanes along with the energy, and the cycle starts over again. When we get into yo-yo cycles such as this, rather than going from strength to strength, the health of the team is damaged.

A faith-filled culture is established when energetic, God-loving people are leading and setting a standard of excellence by serving others, respecting others, and doing life without the silliness, the bickering, and the normal stuff you get when a bunch of people work and do life together. An energetic culture is one in which everyone participates—a culture of life and hope, a culture of great faith and expectancy, a culture where wins are celebrated and failures forgiven. It's a culture where God-encounters bring change and the atmosphere is charged with faith.

Now, I'm certainly not suggesting you get into a works-based theology and wear yourself out trying to become some kind of superhuman leader. However, I do want to peel back the layers to help you see what could infuse *you* and *your team* with energy.

CLARITY

It's easy for people to follow you with enthusiasm when they know where you're going. Our pastor has kept the church focused by restating his vision statement whenever possible. Over years and years, this repetition has helped to maintain clarity and build trust. We know where we're going—the goal hasn't changed—and we are better able to run with that goal in mind. There's energy for the journey.

At any great energy-filled church or successful organization, you'll find that a vision statement is consistently re-presented and declared. As the years go by, heralding the clarity of the statement brings unity, strength, momentum, and energy for the journey.

Our worship teams work hard at clearing the way for others to become involved and to become part of the fabric of the team. We have a high but realistic expectation that everyone will perform with excellence. Clear objectives result in unhindered energy.

An energetic culture is one in which everyone participates—a culture of life and hope, a culture of great faith and expectancy, a culture where wins are celebrated and failures forgiven.

GOOD FOOD

Don't worry. I'm not going into a spiel about health and fitness, although I could. But I will just throw in a bit of advice here. Whenever the busy seasons are approaching, we encourage the team to get plenty of rest, eat well, and exercise. Boring and practical as that sounds, these suggestions are critical to longevity and increased energy levels when extra work is required. I've learned never to presume that people know how to take care of themselves. In this very parentless generation, the practical, simple things are often not taught.

When I talk about good food, I'm especially referring to the spiritual kind. Make sure you are receiving good, solid biblical teaching whenever possible. You can try to pump yourself up without it for a day, a week, a month or even two, but sustainability in energy comes when our spirits have fed upon the living Word of God. True worship starts and ends with Him, and our spirits are energized as we respond to His love and grace. One of the main reasons we meet as "gathered worshipers" is to maintain our unity as one body. Like lightning, the fire of God passes in corporate worship from one body to another to create energy.

JOY

Finding your joy is one thing; keeping it requires connection. Real joy is not circumstance-dependent; it is a fruit of the Spirit— one that God grows in us, and one that I treasure immensely.

Isaiah 60:15 tells us, "I will make you the everlasting pride and the joy of all generations." He is the One who will make you and me the joy of all generations. We can't manufacture joy, but we can stay connected to the One who produces joy within us. Listen to Psalm 16:11: "You will fill me with joy in your presence." Joy is the evidence that Christ is in our hearts.

I like the way Hudson Taylor explained it. He filled a glass of water and placed it on the table before he preached. While speaking, he slammed his fist on the table with such force that some of the water splashed out of the glass and onto the table. He then explained, "You are all going to have trouble at times, but when you do, only what's in you will spill out."

Fill your spirit with God's Word and you will find renewed strength to lead with joy. Joy brings life! It makes others feel safe with you. When I am leading our team, and I enter the room full of

When you don't have joy, you don't have the strength or energy to accomplish your purpose.

joy, the atmosphere becomes charged with a sense of security. No drama queens—or kings—allowed! Consider it all joy.

Nehemiah 8:10 states, "The joy of the Lord is your strength." When you don't have joy, you don't have the strength or energy to accomplish your purpose. No joy . . . no songs, no energy for praise, no energy for life.

CREATIVITY

We were created to be fruitful. So if you're not feeling productive, it could be time to stir up your creativity. Yes, getting creative might take a bit of energy, but as children of the Author of all creation—the One who flung the stars into space, who paints majestic sunsets every night only to paint a new one tomorrow, who intricately and lovingly handcrafted each of us for His pleasure—we shouldn't be surprised at our need to create.

When your leadership role starts out in creative expression but ends up with you becoming a facilitator of rosters and schedules, line-ups, and arrangements . . . mmm . . . I think it's time to switch gears and stoke the creative fires within you!

You have God-given gifts and talents, but they must be used in order to develop. Be diligent in seeking the Lord for new ideas. Take the limits off your abilities, and rest in your Father's presence. Welcome the Holy Spirit into your time. Then, with the splendor of God's creativity pouring through you, you will find the strength to distance your former excellence and start afresh with something even greater. When you delight yourself in the Lord and let Him cultivate His genius in you, the problems that now stifle you will be solved with ease—and you will feel the energy of His life coursing through your veins.

Second Timothy 2:1–7 says, "So, my son, throw yourself

into this work for Christ. Pass on what you heard from me—the whole congregation saying Amen!—to reliable leaders who are competent to teach others. When the going gets rough, take it on the chin with the rest of us, the way Jesus did. A soldier on duty doesn't get caught up in making deals at the marketplace. He concentrates on carrying out orders. An athlete who refuses to play by the rules will never get anywhere. It's the diligent farmer who gets the produce. Think it over. God will make it all plain" (THE MESSAGE).

Benjamin Franklin got it right. So perhaps now it's our time to let our kites soar into the heavens and prove to the world that God's energy can become the liquid fire we need to pass our faith from one body to another. Then we too can alter the way the world receives light, communication, and connection.

"You only lose energy when life becomes dull in your mind. Your mind gets bored and therefore tired of doing nothing. Get interested in something! Get absolutely enthralled in something! Get out of yourself! Be somebody! Do something. The more you lose yourself in something bigger than yourself, the more energy you will have."[2]

Norman Vincent Peale

VALUE FIVE:
THE SQUEEZE

Consider it pure joy, my brothers and sisters, whenever you face trials of many kinds, because you know that the testing of your faith produces perseverance. Let perseverance finish its work so that you may be mature and complete, not lacking anything.
—James 1:2–5

"Consider it pure joy," says James. OK, not my first thought when I face pressure and "the squeeze" is on. But, OK, joy . . . here we come!

It's easy for me to look at your pain and know that you can endure it. But when I'm the one who is suffering, it's a little more difficult to believe that anything good will come of it. So how much pressure is too much? I can think of many giants in the faith who felt the stretch required of them was almost unbearable—to the point of quitting, or even having suicidal thoughts—rather than allowing the momentary pain to produce an inward growth spurt that would eventually catapult them into their God-ordained future.

The reason I've included the squeeze as a value is that I know beyond a shadow of a doubt that when the pressure is on and you feel you simply can't take any more, God is up to something great in you!

Surrender to Joy

Perhaps you've heard of Australia's renowned evangelist Nick Vujicic, who preaches joy in Christ. Born with a rare disorder called Tetra-amelia, he's a limbless young man, missing both arms at shoulder level and legless with two small feet, one of which has two toes. Nick's birth was initially devastating to his parents, but he went on to become one of the greatest blessings in their life.

Nick was bullied mercilessly in school. As an eight-year-old, he had already started contemplating suicide. At age ten, he tried to drown himself in four inches of water, but changed his mind after realizing how his death would hurt his parents, who are pastors of a local church. Nick begged God for new arms and legs. Nothing happened. So Nick finally said yes to the squeeze and began to thank God for his life. At seventeen, he started speaking openly for God and eventually founded his nonprofit organization, Life Without Limbs. Today he's spoken to over three million people in more than twenty-four nations, graduated from a university with two degrees, written a book, been on numerous television shows, and won an award for best actor in the short film *Butterfly Circus*.

Every morning when Nick gets out of bed, he has to overcome the challenge of grooming himself without the aid of hands and feet. It's an ongoing struggle to live in a world of tall people when you have to look them in the knees. Go Nick! You inspire us all.

It's the squeeze we've endured that proves to the world that the final product is worth it.

From Pressure to Perfection

When I think about this value on a musical level, I am reminded of how our team has had to work diligently and endlessly to reach a level of playing that is consistently strong. There's no such thing as simply crossing our fingers and hoping everyone has listened to and practiced the CD at home. We rehearse and rehearse, sometimes late into the night. And we've been doing so for years, simply to ensure that we are representing the Lord with our finest and helping to inspire and facilitate the cry of the human heart in worship. What I've learned is that developing any gift means hard work, but when we put forth the effort—the ordinary—everybody has a chance to become extraordinary.

A culture of hard work never hurt anyone, as long as you have the goal in sight. And as a leader of worship, I am aware that the goal and strength of the church is to include everyone in the great manifesto of praise that has silenced the enemy from the beginning of time.

One of the pitfalls of music ministry is that if you don't rehearse and instead become reliant on the very gifted (who often have no need to rehearse), you cheat those who do need to be developed and mentored. Eventually, your team dwindles in size, and when the gifted leave for something bigger and better, you have to start over. Our team is always growing and making room for more people. We maintain a "replace yourself" model, which means that we are constantly in the training process with as many as we can handle.

I sat in a leadership meeting one day talking over changes that were so, so good. It was suggested that the members of the music team simply attend one service on the weekend, and then serve in another

When we put forth the effort—the ordinary—everybody has a chance to become extraordinary.

It's in the enduring that you find Christ as your pure joy. It's pressure that turns a lemon into lemonade, and it's pressure that turns your mess into a message for His glory. service on the weekend—receiving and serving. It would remove the pressure of having to serve in both services.

But when I became very quiet, someone asked, "Why the contemplative mood?" I explained that although I knew this idea would lighten the load for the team, I had to ask, "Would we still have access to 'the squeeze'?" You see, without some of the pressure we've experienced over the years, I just don't know that we'd be doing what we're doing. The squeeze has given ordinary people like me a chance to see what we're really capable of handling. And my greatest fear would be that those coming behind us would never need to experience the absolute knowledge that if this isn't God, if He doesn't shine here, we may as well go home!

The thought of the squeeze is, for me personally, one of the great faith adventures of the church. It's in the enduring that you find Christ as your pure joy. It's pressure that turns a lemon into lemonade, and it's pressure that turns your mess into a message for His glory.

We live in a world of shortcuts and quick fixes—the lotto generation, waiting for a wad of cash to fall from the sky. Yet in real life, great things grow with time, energy, and care. We develop patience through the waiting . . . and waiting . . . and waiting some more.

Unfortunately, delayed gratification is difficult for this download-now generation. If they can't have it now, or at least soon, they'll try something else. And that same mentality has been slowly seeping into the church. However, all over the world, churches have said no to convenience, making sure they are found in the middle of villages, cities, and the like so no one will miss out.

They start prepping school halls and community centers at four AM, putting chairs out and little PA systems to make church great. And I am so thankful that they do.

Work is nothing new for God's people. For generations, men and women of God have worked hard and defied all odds to bring the gospel to all men. And that's my point: all this preparation means a lot of hard work, being generous with time and resources, working together to see the church be everything she can be—simply stunning.

But to deprive our children and our spiritual children of these building blocks in life means we short-change them in developing tenacity and spiritual muscle. Even though we don't want to create ridiculous hardships for them just to prove a point, eventually they need to feel the weight of responsibility on their shoulders.

Whenever any of us are confronted with a test—a relational issue, a patience issue, a finance issue, a submission issue, whatever it may be—we need to remember that tests help define what we truly believe. They also mature us and shape us into who we are becoming. I have had so many stretching times when the squeeze has left me without answers. In the process, I've had to learn to yield and trust God. I've also learned to be quiet when I feel like saying my piece. God has used His Word to instruct me to know my place and know His heart toward people. His Word assures me that He is in control, even when I feel out of control.

It's our response to the squeeze that matters most.

The Heart of a Champion

Are you very teachable? Flexible? Are you willing to listen or change? Or do you have an opinion set in stone? Good questions to ask yourself! Remember, flexible things are rarely broken—they simply spring back when the stretch is over.

One young guy at church, Jonathon Douglass (or JD), has

been part of Hillsong Church his whole life. And I've watched him grow and shine, and transition from follower to leader with great dignity and strength of character. And much to his parents' credit, they have never allowed their children to shortcut through any of the journey, even though their kids are well known, and well loved, and could probably slip through without any obvious consequences. No, JD and his siblings have learned to carry the load, to follow through, to stay and pack up, to refuse to quit, to lead people by loving and believing in them.

These are the lessons that true champions learn.

If you watch any champion team in training, they don't just "have a go" and hope they'll make it to the top. No, they push themselves to the limit—pushing their bodies, pushing their emotions, pushing their resolve—to see what they are capable of becoming.

And does it hurt? YES and YES and YES!

Would they be key players on a key team without that kind of pressure? NO and NO and NO.

I heard Sy Rogers speak recently about how the seasons in life from a historical viewpoint have also affected the way we parent our children, and subsequently, lead others. Some generations have pushed their kids way too hard and shown no mercy or emotion along the way, raising stoic "get the job done," "don't hug me" children, and "never be seen crying" men. On the other extreme are those who produce molly-coddling babies, wrapping them in cotton wool, trying to protect them from any measure of pain that may edge up alongside them in life.

Remember, flexible things are rarely broken— they simply spring back when the stretch is over.

Neither is ideal, but the story inside the story is: While trying to protect our natural and spiritual kids from everything, we strengthen them for nothing, raise them to hide, and train them to run from conflict. The meeting in the middle is that in order to train them to lead, they have to partake in all that life has to offer, the highs and the lows, yet be given the tools to overcome their trials and share in the seasons of blessing.

While trying to protect our natural and spiritual kids from everything, we strengthen them for nothing, raise them to hide, and train them to run from conflict.

So in endeavoring to raise a strong team rather than a team of spiritual babies, the teaching that came to my heart was simply this:

During the squeeze, learn to stand.

The message of John 15 is that the fulfillment of ministry, which is the reason you were put on this earth, is a direct result of your relationship with Christ. It's about knowing God and bearing fruit. And the critical element of learning how to stand and to remain secure at your post is one of the most powerful pieces of knowledge you can acquire.

Standing while being stretched and squeezed is not easy. We all want to run and hide—anything to take the pressure off. But rather than running, I love the thought of His presence overshadowing me as I stand—covered by His mighty wings.

Develop a Mission Mindset

In times of the squeeze, keep in mind that *you were designed for a mission.*

Acts 20:24 says in essence that the most important thing is that I complete my mission, the work that the Lord Jesus Christ gave me. Our English word *mission* comes from the Latin word for *sending*. We have been sent on a mission—to be part of writing an incredible history, and to be inspirational for others—to be part of breaking ground so that others can partake of an incredible future, and to live purposefully in the moment that is entrusted to us right now. I love that thought of generational consistency. And if we live with strength for the mission, imagine what the next generation will do.

We continue Jesus' mission on earth as we "go and make disciples of all nations" (Matthew 28:19).

When you realize that what you are involved with on earth (part of a team, raising a family, working a job, attending school) is your mission rather than a task, you will have a greater resolve to stand.

Count the cost!

The abandoning agenda, laying down your life, is costly, but oh so wonderful. Jesus prayed, "Not my will, but yours be done" (Luke 22:42). Stop praying self-focused prayers that ask God to bless what you do. The Bible tells us to give ourselves completely to God—every part of our lives—to be tools in His hand, to be used for His good purposes. It's no longer I—but Christ who lives in me.

Decide now that when it gets too hard, you've already decided to pay whatever the cost.

Imagine if every woman who gave birth decided just before the baby was born, "OK, I'm not doing this. Too hard! It's all over."

(Actually, I'm sure I said that right before delivery). But even though birth is painful (massive understatement!), the squeeze produces joy unspeakable. No pain, no gain!

If we live with strength for the mission, imagine what the next generation will do.

When I am running (I use the word *running* loosely!) and it gets hard, everything in me wants to quit. But because I want to improve, I push my body to go a little further each time, to build my strength and stamina. No, it's not easy, but I challenge myself to run that little bit further every time to make sure I am improving.

Likewise, in seasons of shifting and change and challenge, as you remain secure, you have an opportunity to learn to strengthen your spiritual muscles.

Every time you are faced with a choice of standing or drooping, staying or leaving, getting up or staying in bed, flex your muscles. Muscles need to be strengthened, and the only way that will happen is by use. When your mission muscles are strong, God can and will birth incredible things through you.

Father Knows Best

Prayer is the primary way to increase spiritual strength, to maintain joy for the journey, and to have life more abundant. Oswald Chambers says, "Prayer is the vital breath of the Christian, not the thing that makes him alive, but the evidence that He is alive!" It's been said that one *week* without prayer makes a Christian *weak*. So fall on grateful knees every day, regardless of the squeeze, and thank God for His work in you.

I'm reminded of a day when I overheard someone outside my office complaining about how much work he had to do as a volunteer. When I thought about the actual workload, it wasn't much at all. I understood that he was having an "off" day—we all have them! But as I started to walk outside to console him and maybe lighten his workload a bit, I heard the Lord speak to my spirit, saying, "No, I am doing a work in him." So I went out and just thanked him for his hard work and told him how much we appreciated him.

In the end, all I can do as a leader is ask God for the wisdom to make great decisions, and ask for grace when I don't. I have to realize that God's people are in God's hands. They are free to make their own decisions and then deal with the consequences of those choices.

So as a leader, teach people how to stand, how to enjoy hard work for a greater purpose, and above all, how to pray. It's not your job or mine to simply tell people what to do; it's our job to lead them to the Father so they can hear it directly from Him.

Mmmm, going through the squeeze? God is up to something great in you!

"WHEN WE LONG FOR
LIFE WITHOUT
DIFFICULTIES,
REMIND US THAT
OAKS
GROW
STRONG
IN CONTRARY WINDS AND

DIAMONDS
ARE MADE UNDER
PRESSURE."[1]

Peter Marshall

VALUE SIX:
OPEN DOORS

Your job is to speak out on the things that make for solid doctrine. Guide older men into lives of temperance, dignity, and wisdom, into healthy faith, love, and endurance. Guide older women into lives of reverence so they end up as neither gossips nor drunks, but models of goodness. By looking at them, the younger women will know how to love their husbands and children, be virtuous and pure, keep a good house, be good wives. We don't want anyone looking down on God's Message because of their behavior. Also, guide the young men to live disciplined lives.
—Titus 2:1–6
THE MESSAGE

Sometimes when you've been giving out and ministering to people, the energy required can take a huge toll on you, both physically and emotionally. And, because Jesus was fully man, He too became fatigued. During those times of exhaustion, His disciples tried to protect Him by dissuading people from disturbing Him. But Jesus was never too tired for people, especially those who came with childlike trust and faith. The welcome sign was always hanging out in plain view: Come on in! Jesus had an open-door policy, and the door of His heart was open to anyone and everyone, any time or place. So it's not surprising that in Matthew 19, the Lord disregards the advice of His disciples, and we find the little children rushing up to Jesus and climbing onto His lap to stroke His beard, feel His love, and receive His blessing.

As we draw from the life example of Jesus, we find a very important principle in leadership: As much as possible, live with an open-door policy.

Open Doors, Open Lives

It's become more and more important for me personally to maintain an open atmosphere, both in the office and at home, so friends, both new and old, feel welcome to just come on in. Even while working in our church offices, the door has remained open—that is, apart from the first few weeks of a new college term when overseas students would walk past slowly to get a good look in! Sometimes I felt like charging a fee and raising some dollars for missions!

As funny as that sounds, it's become increasingly more apparent that many of the people we are leading, many who are without strong role models in the natural sense, are looking for more than instruction in how to lead a meeting, or how to preach—rather, they are often even more curious about how to live life.

I'll give you an example from an incident that happened years ago. I had just given some introduction for the curriculum and then decided to open up the floor for questions. The staff and I had answered a few nicely packaged queries regarding musical transitions in worship, when an uncomfortable silence fell over the crowd. One of the delegates spoke out, "Can I ask you something of a more personal nature?"

"Sure," I replied, wondering where this question would go.

Being open means being willing to tackle the hard questions, so laying anxiety aside, I let him ask away.

Well, this guy started asking confrontational but healthy questions about the tension he was feeling over balancing the expectations of church leadership with those of home and family. We explained that the purpose of the church is not to create tension in the home, but rather to change us into the likeness of Christ so that He can take first place in our homes.

As leaders, it's our responsibility to care for those we are leading, and we should always consider the fallout from requiring too much of people *before* we ask them to commit. People are often so kindhearted and so wanting to honor God that they will often say yes to ministry and unwittingly neglect home and family. I'm all for throwing people into the deep end, getting them to serve hard, but not at the expense of others.

These real-life questions continue thick and fast to this day. Young people are concerned about marriage and staying married. They want to know how to prevent weariness and how to stay on fire for the things of God. They want to know about finances, cooking, running a home, and even when to have children. They're not afraid to ask tough questions, such as, "What does the Bible say about homosexuality? About divorce? About tithing? About the kingdom of God?" They want to know, and they want to know now!

So the open-door philosophy was born out of a need for mentoring, and continues to this day. Our lives have been available to be read, followed, and questioned. I've also had to arm myself with biblical answers for everyday situations. And I learned quickly that I didn't have to be the expert with all the answers. I simply listen to the Holy Spirit, pray with them, and point them to Christ.

The most important thing we mentors can give is availability. Of course, sometimes God will use us to be part of the

Sometimes God will use us to be part of the problem-solving process by helping others to define the problem and to recognize the options available— but we are not called to control their choices.

problem-solving process by helping others to define the problem and to recognize the options available—but we are *not* called to control their choices. The main thing is to make sure that we have built margins into the day—when needed, on purpose—to be available for those who come with childlike faith and trust.

In the end, it's all about loving the people and being good shepherds. We don't always know what's going on in a person's private world, but when someone asks for support, we need to give it whenever possible. With that said, I know from personal experience that it's not always possible to be there for everyone. Mark and I find it a bit challenging to keep family first while maintaining the open-door policy for others. It's a balancing act that only comes with dependence on the Holy Spirit. However, like the children who climbed up on Jesus' lap for a blessing, most people simply need to know that they are valued enough to actually matter—so it's worth the effort.

And speaking of effort, most connections are the result of choosing to reach out to others. One of the great ways to connect with people is in learning to linger, refusing to be in such a hurry. It's incredible to discover the conversations you'll have when you're not racing out the door after a service, no matter how weary you may be.

I have also learned to simply make eye contact when conversing with others. People feel disrespected and quite small when you look past them to check out what's going on in the background.

Connect!

Let Them See the Real You

The open-door policy means including people in your life. I love to have people in my home, chatting with them while simply doing life. Rather than having more meetings, welcome someone into your home to chat while you putter around the house. Bring someone over to be with you while writing a song, or doing something creative. Let that person accompany you when driving the kids around, going to the airport, or running errands. Make it a point to grab one of the young people who has been asking to have time with you, and get him or her involved in the real world with you.

Without an open-door policy, those we mentor tend to foster erroneous notions about what life looks like for those in leadership. Whether buying groceries, dropping off the dry cleaning, or picking up the kids from school, people literally stop to ask if this is really what I do when I'm not on a platform. Scary stuff! (On my way home from the gym, I stopped at the market, and someone actually asked me as I was grabbing groceries if this is what I really look like! No kidding!) So as worldly imaginations and fascinations with celebrity seep into the church unchallenged, there's a tendency to seek fame over the face of God. And when people develop "larger than life" images of those on the platform, they assume that "ministers" are exonerated from any kind of normalcy, including having to surrender all under the mighty hand of God.

A worldly church culture has been urging us to take control of our own lives, to become masters of our own destinies, to do whatever is necessary to get to the top, and then somehow use the Bible to support our actions. However, the Bible was not written as a handy script to adapt or modify as we see fit.

Eugene Peterson explains: "The Author of the book is writing us into his book, we aren't writing him into ours. We find ourselves in the book as followers of Jesus. Jesus calls us to follow him and we obey."[1]

So we raise and train, and love people to the Lord, according to God's Book. We don't write the outcome for anyone; we simply make ourselves available for God's use. Therefore, dear leader, I ask you . . . is your life the open door that makes others feel accepted and welcomed by God, or has it become a door closed to life? Do you welcome questions, or are you a "Don't go there" type leader? To paraphrase Pastor Bill Hybels, "Who are you when no one's looking?" Does the life you live Monday through Saturday reflect one that God would want others to emulate?

The next generation is looking for leaders to follow. They want to know what healthy boundaries look like and how to put them into place. Let's show them, and then tell them how to live a balanced Christian life. Let's start teaching the practicalities of living.

I recently wrote a morning routine for someone who just couldn't cope with getting on with the day. Too basic, you think? Doesn't relate to how you lead? Think again. When the basics in life are sloppy, other areas of life will follow suit. We need to teach our children—natural or spiritual—how to become disciples. They will need our help in learning the disciplines of godly living, such as reading the Word, developing their gifts, becoming punctual, and taking responsibility for their lives. Actually, the list is endless.

As worldly imaginations and fascinations with celebrity seep into the church unchallenged, there's a tendency to seek fame over the face of God.

On an even more personal level, young believers need to learn how to dress acceptably for all occasions. Many young women today are much more influenced by the fashion industry than by mentors or family, but it only takes a little time and care to teach them how valuable they are. Knowing their value will shape their choices, even in clothing. It's not about style and flair, even though our clothes do represent identity, which is both fine and fun. It is, however, about holiness—that's our standard.

Close the Door on Condemnation

And, dear leader, please don't sit in judgment of young men or women who don't dress or look the way you'd prefer. Spiritual transformation takes place on the inside and then over time, works its way through the whole of our beings. I become very upset when young people are discounted for how they look or judged for what they appear to be by those who don't even know them. It's acceptance that causes people to change, not rejection. God knows exactly who each one of us will become. He sees people from a whole different perspective than we do, because He formed us, cell by cell. He wove within our framework a need *It's acceptance that causes people to change, not rejection.* for himself and a need to accomplish a purpose, and He alone knows what it will take to change our hearts toward Him.

Too many kids today are at odds with both the secular establishment and the churches. They've been so judged, shamed, and rejected that they are afraid to trust. They've grown up in a society that knows very little about commitment, boundaries, and holiness. They long to know the Jesus who befriended prostitutes and tax collectors, the one who welcomed the thief into Paradise and laid down His life for rejected human beings. Show them that kind of Jesus, and there won't be room enough in our churches to contain them all.

Listen to John 4:35: "Don't you have a saying, 'It's still four months until harvest'? I tell you, open your eyes and look at the fields! They are ripe for harvest."

He is telling us to open our eyes—the harvest is here and ready. But the harvest doesn't look like it used to. It is sleeved with tattoos, pierced with nose, lip, and tongue rings, and scarred with needle marks and self-inflicted cuttings. Nonetheless, we love the harvest. And more important, God so loves every single one of them that He gave His very finest to bring redemption to them.

A young woman once asked Mother Teresa if she could join her ministry in Calcutta. Her reply: "Find your own Calcutta. Don't search for God in far-off lands. He is close to you, He is with you." God has placed you right where you are to have kingdom influence. It's time to hang the welcome shingle in plain view and to let others know that the door to your heart is open: Come on in!

"DO ALL THE **GOOD** YOU CAN, BY ALL THE **MEANS** YOU CAN, IN ALL THE **WAYS** YOU CAN, IN ALL THE **PLACES** YOU CAN, AT ALL THE **TIMES** YOU CAN, TO ALL THE **PEOPLE** YOU CAN, AS LONG AS **EVER** YOU CAN."[2]

John Wesley

VALUE SEVEN:
EXCELLENCE

The house I am building has to be the best, for our God is the best, far better than competing gods. But who is capable of building such a structure? Why, the skies—the entire cosmos!—can't begin to contain him. . . . I need your help: Send me a master artisan . . . I know you have lumberjacks experienced in the Lebanon forests. I'll send workers to join your crews to cut plenty of timber—I'm going to need a lot, for this house I'm building is going to be absolutely stunning—a showcase temple!
—2 Chronicles 2:5–9
THE MESSAGE

A showcase temple! When Solomon asked the king of Tyre for laborers to help in constructing a temple for God, only the best would do. The Phoenicians were known as the best builders and architects in the world. They were excellent in skill and creativity, but the temple they created was not great enough to hold the magnitude of God. So God decided to build a temple for himself in the hearts of men, and there He would live and breathe and give us purpose for being. Only a heart that is dedicated solely to Him can know the excellence of God—absolutely stunning—a showcase temple!

So when someone recently asked, "How does one become an excellent worship pastor?" I instinctively thought about skill sets, the musical ability, the anointing, and the calling of God—all the things that people consider necessary for a great music ministry. But the words that eventually spilled out of my heart were quite different: "You have to care . . . and care with all your heart. And the reason why you care is very important."

Caring Is Costly

King David, the most excellent worship pastor of all time, understood the *why* of his care. David suffered the backlash of his disobedience time and time again, but Second Samuel 24:20-24 provides a porthole into his heart:

> Araunah looked up and saw David and his men coming his way; he met them, bowing deeply, honoring the king and saying, "Why has my master the king come to see me?"
> "To buy your threshing floor," said David, "so I can build an altar to God here and put an end to this disaster."
> "Oh," said Araunah, "let my master the king take and sacrifice whatever he wants. Look, here's an ox for the burnt offering and threshing paddles and ox-yokes for fuel—Araunah gives it all to the king! And may God, your God, act in your favor."
> But the king said to Araunah, "No. I've got to buy it from you for a good price; I'm not going to offer God, my God, sacrifices that are no sacrifice" (THE MESSAGE).

Here we gain insight for understanding why David alone was called "a man after [God's] own heart" (1 Samuel 13:14). These Scriptures reveal a heart that was not willing to compromise truth, cheat people, or be stingy in his dealings with God. David knew he had failed much and been forgiven much, but he also had a heart that completely trusted God. And he understood that those who really know the goodness of God do not pursue perfectionism, which only produces fear—they pursue excellence, which is the willingness to risk everything for love of the Lord.

Araunah offered the property and other goods without charge so that David's sacrifice would have cost him nothing, but David refused to offer God anything that did not represent 100 percent of his love and devotion. "I'm not going to offer God, my God, sacrifices that are no sacrifice." David called God, "my God." He understood that you don't value anything that hasn't cost you something, and he was willing to pay any price to worship his God. He didn't sacrifice to appease the eyes of men; he sacrificed because his heart had become a temple big enough for God to occupy. Beautiful!

Those who really know the goodness of God do not pursue perfectionism, which only produces fear—they pursue excellence, which is the willingness to risk everything for love of the Lord.

Our Standard Is Excellence

When the reason why you care is because you care for the things that God values, you will protect the unfolding revelations of God in your midst, you will care about the people entrusted to your shepherding and put them before all other urgent requests, you will care about the theology being taught in worship, and you will care that those anthems of praise are the very best you can offer.

"For God so loved . . . that He gave." God's giving was not out

Less care results in careless worship. of obligation; it was motivated by a love that demanded a response of excellence. Any form of honest leadership requires the leader to teach the most excellent way. Not the easy way, or a shortcut way for a quick-fix compromise, but the way of integrity that sets a standard of excellence.

Some say that *excellence* is a showy word, and it does turn off a lot of people. So *The Message* translation actually uses the word *best*. And I would say that excellence is bringing your best to every day of your journey.

Proverbs 22:29 says, "Do you see someone skilled in their work? They will serve before kings; they will not serve before officials of low rank." In your home, excellence will mean serving, forgiving, respecting, and taking responsibility for your actions so that others can see God's Word demonstrated and practically applied through your example. In your local church and community, excellence will require sensitivity and generosity to the needs of others, time to build relationships, and a willingness to lay down your life so others can get ahead. We go the extra mile because we care. Yes, excellence takes more time, more heart, and more devotion than you and I can muster in our own strength, "but we have this treasure in jars of clay to show that this all-surpassing power is from God and not from us" (2 Corinthians 4:7).

The power of excellence is demonstrated by and through our care. As a worship leader, I care that the worship offered to the Lord will be pure and pleasing in His sight—not showy or "spectacular," but earnest and thoughtful. And I desire to always live in that revelation.

Less care results in careless worship. It might sound good and appease the eyes of onlookers, but without care or integrity attached to your pursuit, the worship will result in sacrifices without sacrifice. And careless worship will not have a lasting effect on people's lives.

So like most of the other values, the why behind the what must be taught and caught. Invest time in sharing your why, your testimony, and your stories. Bring your best to those who need your wisdom. Invest your energy in those you shepherd. Without care, the things of God are reduced to rules and boundaries that make no sense, but with care all things endure.

No Sloppy Agape

Matt Hope and his wife, Mel, are two people who exemplify care for God and care for things with enduring value. They are among our closest friends, a couple we do a lot of life with. A few years ago, Matt and Mel packed up their young family and left for Rwanda, East Africa, as part of the Hope Rwanda project team. Matt oversees homebuilding in the Hope Village, so he brought a whole bunch of builders and laborers to get the momentum going on the ground and to ensure that the construction of the buildings could stand the test of time.

As it turned out, the skilled builders spent most of their time and energy training the unskilled locals. It's not that the locals hadn't built a lot of homes out of necessity; it's just that the homes were not built to last. The task of teaching was long and sometimes painful. One particular wall was erected and pulled down and re-erected four times before it was built correctly—but stability was the result, and care was the driver. In the end, many young Rwandans now have the immense pleasure of knowing that they are building homes that will last long into the future.

When mentoring, please don't make the lessons too easy. Remember, the best things in life require:

Care + time + energy.

Genesis 4 tells the age-old story of Cain and Abel, two brothers who worshiped God with their sacrifices. We're told that the Lord accepted Abel's "choice" offering because he presented God with

When we take our eyes off the Lord, sin knocks at the door of our hearts, desiring to master us—and when possible, it will master those who follow us.

the best he had to give. In contrast, Cain's offering was not his finest, and the Lord would not accept it. The Lord warned Cain: "If you do not do what is right, sin is crouching at your door; it desires to have you, but you must rule over it" (v. 7).

We all need to master our tendency to be careless when presenting our hearts as an offering to God. When we take our eyes off the Lord, sin knocks at the door of our hearts, desiring to master us—and when possible, it will master those who follow us. But there are some things we can do to keep our focus. First and foremost, we must learn to rely on the Holy Spirit's leading to stay connected to God and His people.

Our enemy opposes our worship, our unity, and our holiness, so in the environs of our worship team, we always pray before ministering and never deviate from our commitment to gather, commit, forgive, praise, and pull our hearts together. We remind ourselves that worship is holy—not a show, or mere Christian entertainment. We want people to know the excellence of His love for them so they will never again settle for a counterfeit, competing god.

All That Glitters Is Not Gold

There was a day, not long ago, when I had about four hours of delays at an airport. Now, that's not too unusual for those of us who travel a lot, but definitely not my favorite pastime. So, as any good woman would do, I ventured through the airport shops to check out the buys. And it may not surprise you that I eventually found my way into this little costume jewelry store.

Anyway, I discovered the cutest little watch, which was in the shape of a cross. It had a thick white band, and the edge of the face was covered in fake diamonds. Then I saw the price tag—$20. *Must be a typo!* But no, I checked with the clerk, and sure enough, twenty dollars it was.

After thinking about it for two seconds, I decided the purchase was a good one and walked out with the most "blingy" watch I'd ever seen—twenty dollars well spent.

Well, after about two weeks, it stopped working. *What a rip-off!* So I took my bling to the local watch repairman, who removed the back cover and proceeded to have a little giggle. "I do hope you didn't pay much for this. There's nothing worth fixing in here."

Yes, my cute little piece of timekeeping equipment proved to be useless. It looked good on the outside, really good, but there was nothing on the inside to keep it going.

Can you see where I'm going with this? Excellence for excellence's sake is a trap that starts comparisons. Then, over time, convictions are watered down before we even realize it. Soon we're just copying the copy of a copy that used to have our hearts all over it. There's no best about it.

No Match for Excellence

But we don't have to settle for anything less than best. Daniel 6:1–3 tells the story of a young man with uncompromising trust in the Lord. And because of that trust, Daniel excelled with a success that only comes when our hearts are dedicated solely to God: "Darius reorganized his kingdom. He appointed one hundred twenty governors to administer all the parts of his realm. Over them were three vice-regents, one of whom was Daniel. The governors reported to the vice-regents, who made sure that everything was in order for the king. But Daniel, brimming with spirit and intelligence, so completely outclassed the other vice-regents and governors that the king decided to put him in charge of the whole kingdom" (THE MESSAGE).

One of our highest goals in life should be to have an excellent spirit. And Daniel is our champion example in this regard. Daniel 6 reports that he was put in charge of the whole kingdom because of his excellent spirit.

The world has no match for an excellent spirit—it will outrank any gifting, talent, or charisma. And even though the sacrifices will not be without cost, the results will be a temple that is absolutely stunning, a showcase temple for future generations to model.

"IF YOU ARE GOING TO **ACHIEVE EXCELLENCE** IN **BIG** THINGS, YOU DEVELOP THE **HABIT** IN **LITTLE THINGS.**"[1]

Colin Powell

VALUE **EIGHT:**
HUMILITY

Who is wise and understanding among you? Let them show it by their good life, by deeds done in the humility that comes from wisdom. But if you harbor bitter envy and selfish ambition in your hearts, do not boast about it or deny the truth. Such "wisdom" does not come down from heaven but is earthly, unspiritual, demonic. For where you have envy and selfish ambition, there you find disorder and every evil practice.

—James 3:13–16

James tells us that humility is shown by a good life and by deeds that come from wisdom. Sometimes we don't know how to describe humility, but we know it when we see it. Dr. J. Hudson Taylor is one of those people who had it. His life's message was that we must "move men through God—by prayer". . . and everything he accomplished was the result of trusting God by prayer. If you were to define the word *humility* by Taylor's life, it would be God-confidence. Called by God at seventeen, the young Englishman became the first missionary to inland China, who later founded the China

Inland Mission with more than three hundred stations. He spoke five varieties of Chinese and spent five years translating the Bible into the *Ningpo* dialect.

One story people enjoy telling about him happened when he was asked to speak in Melbourne, Australia, for a large Presbyterian church. After being introduced as a spiritual giant and having his accomplishments recited with glowing accolades before the congregation, Taylor was finally presented as "our illustrious guest." Taylor paused for a moment and then began, "Dear friends, I am the little servant of an illustrious Master." What better way to model humility!

Unmasking Pride

We often think of *humility* as the trait of being modest or respectful. However, I find this definition to be an understated depiction of a character trait so powerful that it transforms those who have been touched by it. The word *humility* actually comes from the root *humus*, meaning clay, earth. It suggests being teachable, flexible, pliable, able to mold or reshape—the clay on the potter's wheel (see Jeremiah 18).

However, as we see in this section's opening Scripture, the absence of humility opens the door to pride, the foundation for envy, selfish ambition, disorder, and every evil practice. Pride and humility, just like darkness and light, have a hard time hanging out together. Actually, without humility, we have very little chance of sustained influence.

When humility is not present, the words "Your kingdom come, on earth, as it is in heaven" become reversed to "My kingdom reign, my will be done, my ambition be supreme—it's my way or the highway!"

You see, pride—which can mask itself ever so slyly and often in the form of self-righteousness or being a "good person"—has always been the downfall of the prominent, so-called successful person. With that said, let's look at what humility is not:

It's not thinking less of yourself than God thinks of you.

It's not putting yourself down.

It's not letting people walk all over you or treat you like garbage.

It's not having no opinion.

It's not allowing yourself to be minimized to fit in.

It's not refusing to be served by others.

It's not always being on the giving end, especially when God wants you to learn how to receive.

Some of these "nots" tie us up in knots of bondage because they are false forms of humility that often stem from other issues, such as low self-esteem and/or the fallout from disappointment or failure. These misbeliefs actually contradict Scripture and violate God's character. So please don't accept these ideas. You are a person of enormous value to God, and He wants you to enjoy being *you*.

In *The Screwtape Letters* (1942), author C. S. Lewis describes a conversation between two demons: Screwtape, the very knowing older demon, and his student Wormwood, the young up-and-coming demon. It's an interesting take on the enemy's strategy (remember, it's fiction!) to trap human beings into believing that a false type of humility—one that is based on pleasing man—is all that is required of a Christian. Their goal is to disarm even the finest people by crippling them with self-doubt and insecurity, keeping their lives small and ineffective. At one point, Wormwood is instructed to convince the Christian that if he wants to be humble, he must believe his talents are less valuable than he believes them to be—it becomes a perfect way to keep him from using those talents to bless God, Screwtape's enemy.

Some strategy, huh? However, in times of transition, many people do get stuck there, either momentarily or, tragically for some, for the rest of their lives. Sadly, these dear people simply cannot overcome the lies that plague their lives with doubt and unbelief. If I'm talking to you or someone you mentor, I want you to know that these thoughts are from the pit of hell itself, and you must not agree with them. Every single time a self-doubting or fearful thought enters your mind, realize it, reject it, and replace it with faith. It only takes a mustard seed worth of faith to grow a tree of life in your heart. So start small, but keep on believing that you can do what God says you can do because "the one who is in you is greater than the one who is in the world" (1 John 4:4).

"Who, Me?" Moments

You are not the only one who has struggled with wondering how God could use you. The stories of God's humble heroes are found in the "Who, me?" examples in the Word.

For example, David was a kindhearted shepherd boy who, even in the eyes of his own father, didn't qualify or measure up. When the line-up of greats among his siblings paraded before Samuel as possible candidates for king, David wasn't included. And yet because God liked the appearance of David's heart—humble, simple, devoted—God himself raised David up and caused what was obvious to the Lord, his pure heart, to be made obvious to man. When God called him forward, David had a "Who, me?" experience. Later, in Second Samuel 7:18-21, David prays an incredible prayer revealing the contents of his heart:

Every single time a self-doubting or fearful thought enters your mind, realize it, reject it, and replace it with faith.

Who am I, my Master God, and what is my family, that you have brought me to this place in life? But that's nothing compared to what's coming, for you've also spoken of my family far into the future, given me a glimpse into tomorrow, my Master God! What can I possibly say in the face of all this? You know me, Master God, just as I am. You've done all this not because of who I am but because of who you are—out of your very heart!—but you've let me in on it (THE MESSAGE).

Pride comes when we distance ourselves from God's Word, God's presence, and God's will.

OK . . . breathe. Let's take a little pride check. Here goes.

You can tell when pride is rising up in you, when your question changes from: "Who, me?" to "Why you?" "Why not *me?*"

David's big trouble started when success and prominence brought about comfort and options—the two enemies of hunger. Before long, David was doing what seemed right in his own eyes, and that sense of entitlement opened the door to disorder and destruction. As in David's case, pride comes when we distance ourselves from God's Word, God's presence, and God's will.

Isaiah 66:2 states, "These are the ones I look on with favor: those who are humble and contrite in spirit, and who tremble at my word." To be humble is to rely upon God's Word for every step of our journey.

Conversely, to be proud simply means that you have an inflated view of yourself. It's relying on self to make decisions rather than consulting God first—so you take the credit for your accomplishments, believing that your efforts have paved your way. It's a slippery slope, but God knows how to bring you back around.

Consider Moses. He started out thinking he could help God deliver the Jewish people from slavery. So one day when he saw an Egyptian soldier beating one of the Hebrews, he looked around to make sure no one was watching and killed the Egyptian. You know the story. Moses was accused of murder and fled to the desert to hide. And God was right there in the desert waiting for him. It was in that desert place, alone with God, where Moses was transformed into a humble man. In fact, Numbers 12 describes Moses as more humble than any other man on the face of the earth. I just love the fact that the Word reveals Moses' struggles with confidence, stuttering as he spoke, never thinking he could be used of God again, especially to deliver a nation—*who, me?* But there you have God's way. He honors the heart of man. In fact, the Lord so trusted in Moses' steadfast, unrelenting, never-turning-back-again heart that He even allowed Moses to see Him and speak with Him face-to-face.

God's Inner Circle

I want God to trust me to speak with him face-to-face, over and over—clearly and simply—until I am trusted to carry within my heart the great mysteries and secrets of His Word.

Don't you want that?

Even though the Word says He will lift those who remain humble, that thought actually doesn't inspire me. But the ability to be trusted with His voice—now that's inspiring! What's more, I think that kind of intimacy is what God intended for each one of us. His will is that you and I would be as humble as Moses so that we are transformed from self-centeredness to God-centeredness. Imagine a church filled with people who simply live to do the will of God and always treat others the way He intended.

Philippians 2:1–11 shares a glimpse of what it might look like:

> If you've gotten anything at all out of following Christ, if his love has made any difference in your life, if being in a community of the Spirit means anything to you, if you have a heart, if you care—then do me a favor: Agree with each other, love each other, be deep-spirited friends. Don't push your way to the front; don't sweet-talk your way to the top. Put yourself aside, and help others get ahead. Don't be

obsessed with getting your own advantage. Forget yourselves long enough to lend a helping hand.

Think of yourselves the way Christ Jesus thought of himself. He had equal status with God but didn't think so much of himself that he had to cling to the advantages of that status no matter what. Not at all. When the time came, he set aside the privileges of deity and took on the status of a slave, became human! Having become human, he stayed human. It was an incredibly humbling process. He didn't claim special privileges. Instead, he lived a selfless, obedient life and then died a selfless, obedient death—and the worst kind of death at that—a crucifixion.

Because of that obedience, God lifted him high and honored him far beyond anyone or anything, ever, so that all created beings in heaven and on earth—even those long ago dead and buried—will bow in worship before this Jesus Christ, and call out in praise that he is the Master of all, to the glorious honor of God the Father (THE MESSAGE).

C. S. Lewis said, "Pride gets no pleasure out of having something, only out of having more of it than the next man. We say that people are proud or rich, or clever, or good looking, but they are not. They are proud of being richer, or cleverer, or better looking than all the others. If everyone else became equally rich, or clever, or good-looking, there would be nothing to be proud about. It is the comparison that makes you proud. The pleasure of being above the rest."[1]

Third John talks about a guy named Diotrephes who was so intent on being prominent and so egotistical that he deliberately stirred up turmoil in the church and blocked John and anyone associated with him from sharing the Word that God had entrusted to them! The desire to be recognized by man destroyed his ability to get into God's inner circle.

Commonalities of the Humble

There are certain things that all humble people seem to have in common, and one of them is:

Servanthood.

Richard Foster writes, "Nothing *disciplines* the inordinate desires of the flesh like service, and nothing *transforms* the desires of the flesh like serving in hiddenness. The flesh whines against service, but screams against hidden service. It strains and pulls for honor and recognition. It will devise subtle, religiously acceptable means to call attention to the service rendered. If we stoutly refuse to give in to this lust of the flesh, that is when we crucify it. Every time we crucify the flesh, we crucify our pride and arrogance."[2]

Keep it simple, friends.

Use your gift to serve others.

Jesus was always focused on others, and He is our example. We need to keep our hearts yielded to the ways of God and keep our mission to live in Him strong and sure, remembering that the Great Commission is all about others.

It's easy to say we are all about others until we get our feelings hurt, or we get overlooked for a recognition we deserved, or someone says something negative behind our backs. That's when we start having "I" trouble, and dying to selfishness is a slow death for the flesh. All I can say is that whenever I feel like one aspect of my flesh has been nailed to the cross, *wow,* along comes another issue to deal with. God knew we would struggle with the flesh, that's why He included so many admonitions about it and even gave us examples of those to follow and those to avoid.

Philippians 2:3 directs us: "Do nothing out of selfish ambition or vain conceit. Rather, in humility value others above yourselves."

And 1 Peter 5:5 instructs us: "Clothe yourselves with humility toward one another."

King David was what we would call a super-celebrity. However, in First Samuel 18:16, we see that "All of Israel and Judah loved David, for he went out and came in before them" (AMP). In other words, he was approachable, not arrogant, but humble, serving others, doing life among the people. And God does life with people too. Isaiah 57:15 confirms this truth: "I live in a high and holy place, but also with the one who is contrite [humble] and lowly in spirit." You can see God in humble people, and there's such a sense of His love and acceptance around them. I'm sure that's how David was, and why the people loved him so.

But according to Psalm 138:6, when God sees us walking in pride, He actually distances himself from us. Therefore, the moment we find ourselves distancing from God and His people, we need to check our hearts.

You and I cannot preach anything that we are not committed to living. The next generation has little time for inconsistencies between what we say and how we live. My own kids have taught me this truth. There have been times when I've taught something to the team, and almost immediately it has been tested in my own life—and *ahhh*, I failed the test! And that's what we love about family—no hiding there!!

Truth is premium, my friends. This is not a show we are putting on called *church*. No, we are the hands and feet of Christ representing Him and all He stands for in our hurting world.

Let's remember that we are the little servants of an illustrious Master.

"Humility is not thinking less of yourself; it is thinking of yourself less."

Rick Warren

VALUE **NINE:**
GREATER THAN ADVERSITY

The world is unprincipled. It's dog-eat-dog out there! The world doesn't fight fair. But we don't live or fight our battles that way— never have and never will. The tools of our trade aren't for marketing or manipulation, but they are for demolishing that entire massively corrupt culture. We use our powerful God-tools for smashing warped philosophies, tearing down barriers erected against the truth of God, fitting every loose thought and emotion and impulse into the structure of life shaped by Christ. Our tools are ready at hand for clearing the ground of every obstruction and building lives of obedience into maturity.
—2 Corinthians 10:3–6
THE MESSAGE

American preacher Billy Sunday (1863 -1935) said, "I know that the devil is real for two reasons: first, because the Bible says so; second, because I've done business with him."

Smart man! You see, most people don't recognize that our enemy's hand is seeding contention, discord, and destruction to start wars among believers and to destroy their hope in God. Someone said, "The devil's cleverest trick is to make people believe he doesn't exist, or that he had nothing to do with our hurts, losses, and suffering." This is why I've included this value as a reminder that there is One greater than any adversity.

Know Your Enemy

A story is told of two little boys discussing the subject of the devil. One boy said to the other, "Do you think the devil is real?" The other replied, "Well, you know who Santa Claus turned out to be. The devil must either be your mom or dad." Funny as that sounds, many people think of their spiritual leaders and sisters and brothers in Christ as the devil instead of coming together and praying that the enemy's schemes be exposed.

Our real enemy is a lack of knowledge for what is truly important and a lack of understanding about how to work together. I've occasionally found myself in the middle of tension with someone, getting really worked up over a matter, when in the end I couldn't even remember exactly what it was all about. That's when I realize that the enemy comes to kill, to steal, and to destroy.

Winston Churchill once said, "If you want to destroy them, distract them." And that's exactly what our adversary does; he distracts us completely from the greater cause, which is to pull together so we might know Christ and make Him known.

Second Corinthians 10:4-5 instructs us to use our passions correctly, to fight in the Spirit realm, "pulling down strongholds, casting down arguments and every high thing that exalts itself against the knowledge of God" (NKJV).

Sometimes we wonder: Is unity possible? Can it really overcome adversity? Psalm 133 says:

> How good and pleasant it is when God's people live together in unity! It is like precious oil poured on the head, running down on the beard, running down on Aaron's beard,

down on the collar of his robe. It is as if the dew of Hermon were falling on Mount Zion. For there the Lord bestows his blessing, even life for evermore (vv. 1-3).

This psalm paints a very real picture of what unity can achieve: First, it brings joy to the Father; second, it brings a witness to the world; third, it brings increased anointing.

However, we've all done business with the devil and encountered situations where no matter how hard we tried, there simply was no resolution. King David knew from experience the disastrous effects of contention between individuals—he himself having to flee from Saul's unrelenting hatred toward him. When you have done all you can in the natural to bring peace, and yet trouble still continues to brew, you need to know how to pray. Life presents us all with situations beyond our control, and we've got to know how to pray for a breakthrough.

Good Out of Evil

Let's remember to pray for those who lead us, to pray for those we lead, to pray for wisdom in each situation, to pray for opportunities for reconciliation. Prayer is the key that opens the gates of heaven. In times of adversity, we can run away from God and let the enemy rule our circumstances or we can run to God and let Him work through our prayers to bring good out of evil.

I stepped up the teaching on this subject with my team after my family encountered a crisis moment that could only be described as terrifying—and we needed God's hand to intervene. It happened when our youngest daughter, Zoe, was five years old. She was at home with us recovering from a tonsillectomy, having had years of repeated tonsil infections. It was a routine operation, and all went well. She was weak, but getting stronger. However, everything changed within a few days; her color was gray, her behavior became strange; she was sleepy and unhappy. I kept taking her to the doctors, but they couldn't find the root of her problem.

Then, about eight days later, in the middle of the night, Mark and I heard this strange noise coming from her room. We ran to Zoe and found her lying in bed hemorrhaging. We called for an ambulance, and then prayed. She was losing a lot of blood quickly, but (praise God!) the ambulance was close by. The ambulance officer was such an incredible man, a Christian. He and his crew raced to one hospital to stabilize her (met by another Christian, a doctor from our own church!). Then, they transferred her to a children's hospital for further treatment (where Christians were seemingly everywhere!). Zoe responded well to treatments, and we were home a few days later—extremely grateful to God and to all those wonderful people who have devoted their lives to the field of medicine.

Our church was caring and gracious and really looked after us. Our church kids' mascot, Max, even popped in for a visit. To be on the receiving end of pastoral care was certainly humbling but oh so appreciated.

Interestingly, in the days and weeks that followed, I was surprised at the responses from some of our young team, concerned and loving of course, but the questions that arose went like this: How did you pray? What kind of words did you use when you prayed? Were you in a panic? Is it OK to panic in a crisis? Does panic mean we have no faith?

I finally realized how important it is that we teach on the grassroots issues of Christianity. Like I said in Open Doors (Value Six), the questions were intense: How do we pray in times of strife? Or when life feels like it's falling apart? What does an authentic Christian life look like? If you haven't got it "all together," can you still be the real deal?

And so, when I returned to our weekly rehearsals and teaching nights, I started to speak a little about spiritual warfare, what the Bible says about prayer, and how to trust God for miracles even when all hell seems to be unleashed over your world. We are growing continually in these areas of praying the Word, bringing intentional spiritual answers to our every need.

Leadership teaching is most effective when it's been tested, tried, walked-out, and modeled in your life first.

Leadership teaching is most effective when it's been tested, tried, walked-out, and modeled in your life first. Then it becomes part of the tapestry of who you are so that all can see the handiwork of God in your life.

Of course, not every situation has a happy ending. We have prayed and believed for people to be healed, but the healing did not occur here on earth. Sometimes disputes have erupted and, even with help, there was no resolution. Sadly, we've stood with some remarkable young people as their parents have gone through the hell of divorce, using their kids as bargaining chips, their little hearts being broken and crushed. And so we need to teach people how to approach adversity and trouble in ways that help them to stand strong, to speak aloud the promises of God's Word, and to decree the kingdom of God over every situation.

I have included the following study on Psalm 46, because it really helped our team members to cement their understanding of how to walk through fiery trials without being burned.

Psalm 46 Study

For the director of music. Of the sons of Korah. According to *alamoth*. A song.

[1] God is our refuge and strength, an ever-present help in trouble.

² Therefore we will not fear, though the earth give way and the mountains fall into the heart of the sea,
³ Though its waters roar and foam and the mountains quake with their surging.
⁴ There is a river whose streams make glad the city of God, the holy place where the Most High dwells.
⁵ God is within her, she will not fall; God will help her at break of day.
⁶ Nations are in uproar, kingdoms fall; he lifts his voice, the earth melts.
⁷ The Lord Almighty is with us; the God of Jacob is our fortress.
⁸ Come and see what the Lord has done, the desolations he has brought on the earth.
⁹ He makes wars cease to the ends of the earth. He breaks the bow and shatters the spear; he burns the shields with fire.
¹⁰ He says, "Be still, and know that I am God; I will be exalted among the nations, I will be exalted in the earth."
¹¹ The Lord Almighty is with us; the God of Jacob is our fortress.

Psalm 46 is addressed to the chief musician, and I love how the Word of God puts value on the highly skilled in the areas of music and arts. In First Chronicles 15:20, we read that Zechariah, Eliab, and Benaiah were to praise the Lord with "psalteries on Alamoth" (KJV). As far as I can tell, psalteries on Alamoth (*Alamoth* is defined as "virgin," or untouched by the flesh) may mean worship with fresh sounds in the Spirit rather than by old habit or by falling into the trap of singing in only one key. Instead, we are to bring worship with intelligence, joy, and thankfulness, to craft praises that appropriately express the fullness of the occasion. This explanation may not be completely accurate as the information available is scarce, but one thing is certain: these ancient descriptions show that care, time, and skill should be used when bringing a song to honor our King.

The first two words in this psalm, again bring so much

confidence—"God is" . . . our refuge, our strength, our ever-present help.

God is. Do you actually believe beyond a shadow of a doubt that God is all He says He is? I truly believe that if you and I fully grasped this revelation of who God is our lives would look extremely different.

God alone is our all and all, our strength in weakness and a very present help.

I was in worship at a funeral for one of the dear brothers in our church. Yes, it was sad. And yes, there was grief and heartache, but I had an overwhelming sense of God's *very present* help—closer than your closest friend or relative, and even more present than the trouble itself.

I'll never forget when just after my dad died, I had a sense of sadness that was way too much to bear. Dad and I were exceptionally close. I was his buddy, and even though life for him at the end was very confusing, he had Christ, and in that knowing, he had everything. Losing him was like losing my center. Weeks later I still thought I might die of heartache. Then one day I was talking to God while hanging clothes on the clothesline—actually, I wasn't talking to God, I was crying out to Him—when suddenly, I literally felt His mighty arm wrap around my shoulder to comfort me . . . very present, coming at just the right time. I didn't want to move, or breathe, or mess with that holy moment.

I share this private moment with you to encourage you today that God alone is our way through the trial. Though many trials will try to defeat us—adversity at its evil best—we can stand strong, knowing our God is near. Even when heaven and earth pass away, even then, God is!

Listen to this: "Evil may ferment, wrath may boil, and pride may foam, but the brave heart of Holy confidence trembles not" (Spurgeon, of course!).[1]

We then find a *Selah* . . . meaning: pause, be calm, think for a moment.

The music set to Psalm 46 must have been quite colorful because the words are so heartrending. After such a musical interpretation, the psalmist indeed would have needed to take a deep breath to bring calm, and to reflect for a moment. This pause is not the fruit of dismay or doubt but merely a time to re-tune, to set your instrument for the deliberate music of victory in the midst of a storm and then make ready for the music of the overcomers.

Now we are at the river, whose streams make glad the City of God, Zion, whose streams are not intermittent, but ever-flowing with grace and favor—rivers of life and joy, supplying all of our needs, bringing life and refreshing. The church is like the City of God. It receives His design, His glory, His purpose, His people, His message, His provision. Streams of life run from it—dedicated to His praise and glorified by His presence.

The City of God has always caused the enemy to rage, so it should come as no surprise that the Word says the heathen get angry about the streams of life. "How did this happen?" they continually ask. Their angry cries tend to swell in volume and intensity. And then, beautifully, the Lord utters His voice, and the earth melts! God is!

"Come and see," the psalmist declares. Come and see what God did to overthrow our enemies . . . our strength and shield, our ever-present help. He was faithful yet again to His Word and to His character. There's talk of what the powerful voice of the Lord can achieve: peace to war, end to strife, crushing even the greatest of enemies until they cannot wreak havoc ever again. One word from God is all it takes to still the storm, and that's why the Word of God must be in you. His Word is your sword to cut down the enemy. Your greatest defense is in praying God's Word.

Then, the words we all know and so value: "Be still, and know that I am God." The great I am says to you, "Remember, I am."

He will be exalted among the heathen and exalted on the earth.

Why then, do we hesitate to trust in our God, the great I am?

If you truly trust, you must stop trying to work everything out yourself.

Trust is putting our confidence in something, relying on it.

Learn to let go, and trust God.

I found the following song by the great reformer Martin Luther:[2]

> A sure Stronghold our God is He,
> A timely shield and weapon;
> Our help He'll be and set us free,
> From every ill can happen.

> And were the world with devils filled,
> All eager to devour us,
> Our souls to fear shall little yield,
> They cannot overpower us.

Luther's explanation of Psalm 46 is: "We sing this Psalm to the praise of God, because God is with us, and powerfully and miraculously preserves and defends His Church and His Word, against all fanatical spirits, against the gates of hell, against the implacable hatred of the devil, and against all the assaults of the world, the flesh and sin."

So I leave you with this thought: God is.

"The greatest glory in living lies not in never falling but in rising every time we fall."

Nelson Mandela

VALUE TEN:
FAILURE IS NOT FINAL

Love never fails.
—*1 Corinthians 13:8*

In other words, if at first you don't succeed, try, try again!
I remember my mum saying this to me when I was a
little girl. (Funny what you remember as you get older!)
These days, I like to say, "If at first you don't succeed,
keep on trying, because God's love for you will *never* fail."

Basically, the core of this value is: Never write people
off for making a mistake! God does not work this way,
and neither should we. God moves in our lives to change
us, but He doesn't move on and leave us behind when we
let Him down. No, He is committed to every single one of
us. I thank the Lord for not writing me off or condemning
me to life in the desert for my mistakes, and I'm sure you,
dear leader, can say the same thing. It's called grace—the
sovereign message that silences condemnation and brings to
the forefront the reason for the cross.

Oh, how we all need grace. Too many people have shared

experiences with me of trying to step out into something new, and when they failed, not only did they lose their own confidence but also the confidence of their peers. And it's only natural to be disappointed in ourselves when we've set a goal and missed it. However, the experience can be quite embarrassing, especially when we have to admit our failure to those we hold in high esteem. But let's remember that failure can be one of God's most effective teaching tools for building character.

Freedom Is a Way-Back Plan

One of the great lessons I've learned in dealing with people who have made mistakes by trying the untried, making a bad decision, or dropping the ball is that we leaders must put the ball back in their hands quickly—with great gentleness, compassion, and wise direction for making a better choice in the future. All criticism should be given with constructive words, never destructive labels. We need to look for the potential in those we mentor and provide a way-back plan for all who fall short of expectations. (Sounds to me like the message of Jesus!)

The leaders of Disney—some of the most successful, creative, fun facilitators in the world—have always told the creative staff, "Failing is good, as long as it doesn't become a habit." What freedom! What a great way to provide an environment where people feel released to "have a go," or try something new, without being "written off" when their ideas don't work out. Mentors, teach your people how to recover from failure. When public blunders happen, whether large or small, they can have such devastating impact that people often abandon the path of their dreams forever!

One trait I so appreciate about God is the way He keeps hanging in there

All criticism should be given with constructive words, never destructive labels.

with His people, even when they mess up big time. For example, while reading Deuteronomy 9 and 10, I was captivated by the events that happened when God gave Moses the Ten Commandments on those two tablets of stone. God himself actually stretched His hand through the heavens and used His finger to write His intent for humankind on those tablets. (Can you even imagine?! I would love to see God's handwriting!)

Anyway, after forty days and forty nights on the mountain with God, the stone tablets were finally handed over to Moses. However in Moses' absence, the people of Israel had gone crazy, behaving corruptly and making carved images of empty gods to worship. And God got angry! He told Moses He was going to destroy the people because they were so rebellious and self-serving.

Moses got angry too! So angry, in fact, that he (can you believe this?) actually threw the two tablets of stone to the ground and broke them! Yikes! But Moses prayed and prayed until he captured God's attention (Deuteronomy 9:19 says the Lord listened to Moses—how lovely is that?) and changed the course of history for those undeserving people. Talk about intercepting heaven and earth! But . . . what astonished me most is that Moses actually threw those hand-engraved-by-God stones on the ground!

Have you ever broken something of great value and regretted it? I remember when a friend dropped in for coffee, and just as he was leaving, the folder he was carrying accidentally snagged the corner of a cloth on a side table. No problem, *except* that the antique tea set Mark had bought me when we became engaged was sitting on that cloth. It was beautiful, handmade, delicate, one of a kind. You guessed it—the whole set fell to the floor and shattered. We all stood there looking at each other with our mouths open. Our friend began to apologize profusely, and of course we said, "No problem." But when he left, I had a little cry.

125

Poor guy. He felt so bad! And I felt bad for him too . . . oh that sinking feeling—mmm. I wonder how Moses felt? Oops! Just dropped (I mean, threw!) the Ten Commandments.

Anyway, in Deuteronomy 10, the Lord fixes it all—the ultimate let's-get-back-on-track plan—and says to Moses, "Hew two tables of stone like the first and come up to Me on the mountain and make an ark of wood. And I will write on the tables the words that were on the first tables *which you broke*, and you shall put them in the ark" (Deuteronomy 10:1-2 AMP, emphasis added).

So here we have the ultimate second chance moment for this time in history. Moses has already broken the first set of stones. Now the Lord says in essence, "Here's a new set, just like the first, but build a box to put them in for safekeeping!"

Notice that God did not ignore the fact that Moses had made the mistake. He simply gave him a way to save face and start again. Ha! God is the ultimate Father at all times—and oh so practical! But I love that Moses himself was not destroyed, just given a better way to do the same thing again. The heart of the Father is always to put us back on track, a little wiser, and ever grateful for another chance.

When you see people repeatedly making unhealthy choices—please, leader—have the courage to sit down with them, take the time to listen and to show the loving concern of the Lord to get back on track. In platform ministry, when someone slips up, says something crazy, makes a musical blunder, we talk about it in a healthy setting, get to it quickly, and restore confidence. If mistakes are not addressed quickly, a small, imperfect moment can become a huge prickle in someone's soul. As is the way of life, small issues, when not confronted at the outset, can turn into huge issues that are much harder to deal with later.

We Can't Out-Sin God's Love

And when someone is making very unhealthy choices that affect his or her soul, family, or walk with God, again, find the strength and time to talk through the issues and have a plan ready to help restore the person. We need to correct others without undermining their will to try again. We need to teach them that it's never too late to start doing the right thing. That's why I placed the Scripture from First Corinthians 13 at the start of this chapter. Even when we fail—love never fails.

We are not here to judge, to condemn, to criticize, or even to know all the details, but we are here to love, encourage, lift up, pray, and be supportive when resolve is weak. Jesus is called the Rock—the rock of our salvation—meaning that He provides *stability* when our lives are tipping out of balance. He provides the *strength* to get up when we've fallen and made a fool of ourselves, and He brings us to *resolution* when we cry out to Him for direction. In being like Him, we too can be a sense of stability when the storms of life are threatening to topple someone's life. We too can reach out to those who need help getting up. And when others have lost their way, we can be a lighthouse to guide them safely back to Jesus.

King David, the great worshiper, committed adultery with Bathsheba and then arranged for the murder of her husband. I'd say that's a pretty big failure! But when David humbled himself, repented of his sin, and sought purity of heart—God heard his cry. And what's more, the great warrior worshiper was revealed as just a "regular kind of guy" who needed God and learned to lean on Him completely. David still had to bear the fruit of that shocking season in his life, but the story of God's redeeming love and David's heart for God is what we remember most about his life. Luke 7:47 tells us that the person who has

Even when we fail—love never fails.

127

been forgiven much loves much, and no one could have loved God more—just read the Psalms. These songs of worship came from a life that made it through the valley of the shadow of death and learned to be so trusting and transparent with God that He called David a man after His own heart. The Psalms are a lasting testimony to you and me and those we mentor that God's love never fails.

First Samuel 16:7 says that "the Lord sees not as man sees, for man looks on the outward appearance, but the Lord looks on the heart" (AMP).

See, God is looking for repentance, which invokes true change. Repentance is the recognition that we are willing to trust His character, receive His love, and come under the protection of that love, no matter what the cost to change. And His love never fails to change us.

Love Triumphs Over Defeat

The Father's love is so incredible. My favorite story and picture of His costly love is found in the story of the prodigal son. This son had wasted his inheritance on worldly living, turned his back on the family, and disappointed his dad, but the heart of his father was always on the lookout, poised and ready for the son's return. Even before the son came home, his mistakes were already swallowed up in the love of his dad.

In the same way, the Lord saw us wasting our precious lives and came down to be to us like this father, who—even as the boy was a long way off—saw him, ran to him, and fell on him and kissed his neck. It was the boy from the pigpen, the one many wouldn't get close to because they couldn't get past the smell to see who he really was: a human being filled with the promise of God.

But his father's love was too strong to fail. The son stands before his dad with the stench of wrong decision all over him, and the father clothes him with the finest of everything, puts on a party, and welcomes him home.

Anyone can walk others through the good times, but true leaders know how to walk people through the wilderness and show them how to stand strong in the hard times.

"He looked beyond my faults and saw my need." I wrote these words in a song many years ago after reading Psalm 18. It blew me away to think of God's commitment to us—to respond to our cries, and when we're in trouble, to be right there to handle our case.

Sometimes He moves heaven and earth to intervene; other times He brings the answers through ordinary people like you and me. If we stand aloof with those who are stepping out in faith by judging their immature decisions and icing them out when they make mistakes, then we shouldn't call ourselves leaders. Anyone can walk others through the good times, but true leaders know how to walk people through the wilderness and show them how to stand strong in the hard times.

It's like parenting. The most wonderful and overwhelming privilege on the planet is to be entrusted to shape these lovely little lives. But I can also tell you it is the most heart-wrenching, emotionally exhausting, hard work there is.

How will people know we are worthy of following? John 13:35 explains: "By this everyone will know that you are my disciples, if you love one another."

Love is a big word—an action word, which means it will require effort on your part. For Jesus, love meant sacrifice, so we should not be surprised to learn that leading God's way means loving God's way, the way of sacrifice. Some of the people you and I love have the potential to be dangerous to themselves, to you, to your team, and to the church. And we can't do anything without God's wisdom, not even love. But we can trust the Word of God and the power of prayer to show us how to cover them and help them to get the healing they need. I must admit that I've been absolutely shocked by the "secret" behaviors of some people. God may have us stand with them for weeks, months, or years, or He may want us to direct them to one of the community-based services that offers professional help, help that the church is unequipped to provide. Remember, you don't need to have all the answers.

Learn to Laugh

Sometimes, loving someone through a mistake simply requires a hug, a giggle, and an "it will all be fine, mate" response. Most people just need to know that they will never be discounted and that they can still laugh, even in the midst of failure. As a leader, a sense of humor is a must, and if you don't have one, it's time to start developing this part of your personality. It makes life so much easier for everyone. Even in the worst of circumstances, humor can help us see things from a new perspective. Consider Thomas Edison's plight.

Known as the father of the electrical age, Edison knew God. It's been said that when the elderly Edison's laboratory caught fire, destroying millions of dollars worth of equipment and a lifetime's worth of work, he told his son to run and get his mother because she would never have an opportunity to see anything like it again. Later, walking through the ashes, he told her, "All our mistakes are burned up. Thank God we can start again." What a sense of humor!

The last few years we have worked closely with Dave and Joyce Meyer, leading the worship for some of their events and mission endeavors. We consider it a huge honor. They are a great couple, and they truly are who they present themselves to be.

With that said, we were leading worship at a conference for the

Meyerses in Nashville, and having one of those amazing meetings where you seriously feel like heaven has invaded the room with a liberty to worship that brings real freedom and joy. The members on my team are a part of our church and they have traveled with me so many years that we have a certain flow and trust we lean into when playing. So at a critical moment during one of the songs, I called for a key change (a musical lift), but only half the band saw my signal. The other half didn't. The music was loud and confident and heading for such a powerful crescendo and . . . *#!*#! You guessed it! We hit with cyclonic strength a crescendo of musical mess played with such confidence and volume that I think even the stars in the sky made a slight adjustment!

After a moment of recovery, we nervously laughed, waved good-bye to the Holy Spirit (just joking!), and kept on playing. Later I commented, "Well, maybe people didn't notice." The band just looked at me and said, "Darls, we're in Nashville!" (It's the music capital of the world.) And sadly, with MySpace videos, it was no time before many others saw our musical debacle. (At least these moments have a powerful way of keeping our pride in check!)

As bad as that incident was, in the scheme of things, it's now only a really bad memory! Long ago, I don't think it would have slipped through my soul so easily. I would have beaten myself up emotionally for not leading the band well and for disappointing the people who had invited us. But thank God for a little bit of maturity, time, and a sense of humor. Now I can even write about it, laugh about it, and just smile at God's sense of humor to use my life at all!

On one occasion, I was speaking at the Billy Graham Training Center in Asheville, North Carolina, and right at a pivotal, passionate moment, my shoe caught on the hem of my jeans. Yes, I literally fell flat on my face! The band was sitting there not knowing whether to laugh or cry when one of the guitarists turned to the production manager and said, and I quote, "Should we go help her?" "No," he answered. "She doesn't like fuss. But I'll just go quickly and make sure I got it on video!"

We laughed so hard that night (and so did everyone else who was there). I'm actually getting embarrassed again just typing this into my computer!

These kinds of mistakes hurt our pride rather than our future. So as leaders, our ability to get back up and keep laughing is the only way to show others that they can too.

As a leader, I've made incorrect choices in putting people on the platform to minister when their life choices were not honoring to God. I've also been too hard on people, making the entry point for service too high. But I now know that as long as you are able to admit your mistakes, ask for forgiveness, and have a heart to gather and not condemn—as long as you truly know that God is all about the heart and not about the gift—as long as you are all about inclusion and not exclusion, then everything will be all right. Let's thank God for the Holy Spirit's leading and guiding, teaching and speaking. Where would any of us be without God's friendship and unfailing love?

First Peter 4:8 says, "Above all, love each other deeply, because love covers over a multitude of sins." Failure is not final when it's covered by love.

"**HISTORY** HAS DEMONSTRATED THAT THE MOST **NOTABLE WINNERS...WON** BECAUSE THEY REFUSED TO BECOME **DISCOURAGED** BY **THEIR DEFEATS.**"

B. C. Forbes

VALUE **ELEVEN:**
THROW OUT THE OLD?

God's Spirit spoke through me, his words took shape on my tongue.
The God of Israel spoke to me, Israel's Rock-Mountain said,
"Whoever governs fairly and well, who rules in the Fear-of-
God, is like first light at daybreak without a cloud in the sky,
like green grass carpeting earth, glistening under fresh rain."
                                                  —2 Samuel 23:3–4
                                                  THE MESSAGE

These words from Second Samuel are the last spoken by
King David as he readies himself for the ultimate handover
of leadership. Facing death, we find him exalting God,
edifying the next generation, and stressing the importance
of God-fearing leadership. He goes on to say that God's
kind of leadership is always fresh and life-giving. David is
not threatened that someone might do it better. God has
picked the right man for this time in history. Both David and
his successor would hold the same position, but they would
rule differently. David had been a man of war; Solomon would
be a man of peace. David spent his life gathering and making

plans to build the temple; Solomon would take it to the next level and see what David had only envisioned. David's transfer of leadership was not the end but the ongoing of his influence. He was transferring the old to make it fresh and life-giving for the new generation.

Change can be difficult when you're right in the middle of the "shift."

"Out with the old, in with the new," I jokingly said to some of the guys who had been part of our team for a long time. We all laughed nervously, but I left church that day with a nagging sense that God wanted to put the axe to the roots of my own insecurities. In turning over my leadership on the platform to make room for others, it was easy to fall into the trap of feeling that the new team might outshine ours. No one wants to feel that he or she can be easily replaced or that what has been given will be tossed aside. Mmmm, Lord, help me. Forgive me.

As I began to make the choice to starve my flesh and become the leader God intended, I realized that my identity was not in my leading but in my relationship with God. I also understood that just like good parents, leaders with a kingdom focus desire more success for their spiritual offspring than they themselves have had. Life-giving mentors celebrate when the younger ones outshine them. As management expert Robert Townsend said, "True leadership must be for the benefit of the followers, not the enrichment of the leaders."

Root Your Identity in God

History proves that many who approach a change of season in leadership are not secure enough in their own identity to let go and trust God to use them in a new way. Instead of having a kingdom focus to bring through "next gen-ers," they become offended, critical, and defensive. So they end up jumping ship too early and ridiculing the process, complaining about the way the rising generation brings in change.

"True leadership must be for the benefit of the followers, not the enrichment of the leaders."

Some people hold on to a position or title for dear life; they hold on so tight, in fact, that they sabotage their own lives in the process. I've watched people leave in such a flurry of drama that they not only hurt those who still needed their coaching but they also ambush their own next powerful season with God.

If you are feeling the winds of change in what you are leading, my advice is to make sure that you have your identity rooted in God's purposes and plans, not your own. Then you can lead the process with strength. Please don't jump ship when you see others questioning the status quo and dreaming of new possibilities. Be a gracious captain until the ship is stable. Yes, the new will look different and sound different from what you have known and preferred, but that doesn't mean it is less heartfelt or God-honoring.

The rumblings in your emotions can be a call to seek the Lord and ask Him to heal the insecurities in your own heart. Proverbs 1:33 says, "But whoever listens to me will live in safety and be at ease, without fear of harm."

The enemy takes delight in destroying the territory of the soul, and negative thoughts about oneself left unchallenged and un-dealt with will eventually take you out of your own race. God's Word tells us to "[thoroughly] examine" ourselves (1 Corinthians 11:28 AMP). It is the Lord's privilege to lift one man up and remove another. But He doesn't throw us away like an old piece of clothing. No, He takes us from "one degree of glory to another" (2 Corinthians 3:18 AMP).

I have a friend so disciplined in her wardrobe that when it comes to "out with the old," if she purchases something new, she *always* gives or throws away whatever she is replacing. It's a fantastic way to keep your home organized, but does not translate into dealing with people! When we treat people like commodities, we damage them and dishonor God.

If the only time people ever hear from you is when you want something from them, it's no mystery why you would find it hard to gather the troops. You and I can't love those we don't know and value, and leadership that is not based on love won't endure. People need to be cared for and brought forward in their gifts, talents, and abilities to establish new contexts in the church, not to promote the leader.

The strength and beauty of the church has always been her passion to love people, to create a sense of safety, and to shine even in the darkest places. The church is known for her diversity, her ability to embrace every single person. She is unique! She is represented in every nation, tribe, and tongue—a combination of wisdom and enthusiasm, experience and naïveté. The older speak life and lessons to the younger, and the younger bring new energy and enthusiasm, pioneering a new way.

Talk It Through

When the time comes for a shift to happen—in whatever way, shape, or form—there does not have to be bloodshed or an abrupt ending that leaves people wondering what happened and why. It's the lack of truthful communication that leaves people in the dark, causing their hearts to respond with disappointment and fear. Leaders, I urge you to keep the lines of communication open. Be forthright, honest, and worthy of trust.

So let's talk about communication. What's not to say?

Try sustaining a marriage without communication and it won't work for long. Try raising your children without communication and you'll have kids whose value-forming years are the result of the loudest voice in their world (which is sometimes the television).

You cannot have an alive and sustaining relationship with God without communication and prayer; you will end up feeling like heaven is very silent.

Smooth transitions are always dependent on thoughtful process and thoughtful language. God has placed such a high priority on communication that He calls himself the Word.

And the heroes of faith understood the importance of communication too. Deuteronomy 33 tells the story of Moses' last days. When he realizes that this will be his last opportunity to communicate with the people he has led for so long, he speaks absolute and wholehearted blessing over them. In verse 6, he starts naming the tribes, and spends his last moments on earth pouring into their future, speaking the Word of God and the heart of a father over every one of them. He holds nothing back in expressing his love for God and people.

Leadership is about example, vision, hope, and legacy. It's not just talking the talk, but walking the walk. Moses was so loved that after he died in the land of Moab, the people wept over his passing for thirty days.

Speak Greatness, See Greatness

It was when I began to speak into and invest in the dreams of others that I began to change my own speech. As I called others forth in blessing and vision for the future, I found myself raising the bar in speaking my own visions and dreams into the realm of possibility. It took an inner adjustment and a greater trust in God, but now what seemed to be impossible when I first started has become quite possible— and I am ready to stretch for more. I think the reason we often get stuck

Smooth transitions are always dependent on thoughtful process and thoughtful language.

is that we forget our need to shake out of the old and embrace the new.

One Christian leader said to me, "Good on you, Darls. Better you making the changes than having them done to you!" Amen to that!

And so as leaders, very much on purpose, we need to start lifting up our own language and speaking with more energy about solutions rather than problems. We need to speak about leading nations and not only our communities. We need to speak about seeing miracles, not just dreaming about them as a concept for the future. Let's start disciplining ourselves to live with renewed vigor and passion, using whatever God has placed in our hands.

That's what we did, and it didn't take long for the atmosphere over our team and each of us as individuals to start to lift in every way—and it has been so infectious!

The fun part of this choice has been watching others enter this fresh, life-giving environment and wanting to embrace it (it is stimulating) and adopt it as their own way of transmitting faith from one generation to another.

One of the great advantages of this make-room-for-the-new mindset is that it definitely strengthens one's resolve to launch into some brave and unchartered waters. But God's Word is full of great stories about ordinary men and women who knew their own inadequacies and yet believed in God's ability to use them for something greater. They got there by believing in that still, small voice that says, "You can do it!"—even when all evidence tells you otherwise. And that's how we will get there too.

And so the legacy of the undone begins in your bloodline.

Earlier in the book, I mentioned my grandparents. They are devoted, passionate Christians, who in their late nineties

We need to speak about seeing miracles, not just dreaming about them.

are still dreaming, still living independently, still driving (ahhh!), and still encouraging all their kids, grandkids, and great-grandkids in the ways of God.

Nan was in her eighties when she had an encounter with the Holy Spirit that changed her forever, even though both she and Pop had been Christians since they were young.

They stand at the doors of their home church each weekend and help to look after the "old people." They still send us gifts at Christmas, and take the time to call wherever we may be to encourage us in our faith and speak blessings over us. Each time they call, they speak as if it would be the last time, and it's their commitment to create a smooth transition that I admire most.

The last time my Pop saw my second daughter, Chloe, who is very passionate about architecture, he hugged her and let her know that, even though he wouldn't be here physically for the opening of her first building, he is so very proud of her. What a kind man. No regrets, no withholding love when it helps to define a young person's dreams, no speaking negatively over the future and the world in which our children are growing up. Just speaking the Word of God and His promises over us and all that is in our hearts.

My Nan faithfully played the organ in church for many years, but when the time came to give it up, she graciously said, "Time for the young ones." Now, that's generosity at its purist. It's the old loving the young and being the bridge to their dreams.

I know it really encourages some of the younger ones on our team to have me there challenging them—still leading worship, still writing, dreaming, and creating—but more often just standing to the side and cheering others on as they take their leadership place. Sometimes I have had to swallow my pride and tackle my own thought processes on the journey, but the end result is so worth it.

Cultivate Roots and Wings

When we invest in others for the long haul, a wonderful sense of trust and friendship develops over time. Sadly, I believe many people miss out on this incredible gift because they don't stick around long enough, or they leave their posts at the first sign of conflict. Conflict is inevitable when doing life with people! God did not create us to be robots, but human beings with thoughts and feelings and a need to be heard. So conversation is premium. Loving conversations are not the result of forcing our opinions on others but rather of dying to self and preferring others.

Matthew 5:9 says, "Blessed are the peacemakers, for they will be called the sons of God."

I understand that people do need to move on. Leaving can be a healthy thing, but when the leaving happens because of unresolved conflicts, the problems simply go with us.

To be honest, I love knowing that I have helped someone develop the wings to fly, because in doing so the kingdom of God is multiplied and strengthened. And it's also wonderful to know that I have had a part in making room for someone else in leadership. However, that doesn't mean I haven't had my share of heartaches. At times, I've begged, challenged, and tried in my own strength to instill a sense of worth in those I knew had the potential to lead, but when it didn't happen their way or in their timing, they left anyway.

Sometimes people transition well; sometimes they don't. In the end, it's their own decision, their own choice. As a leader, you can only do so much. Everything under heaven has a time and season, but some people lack the wisdom to discern their seasons.

I honestly think it is much easier, short term, to simply walk away and become one of the "misunderstood ones" than to endure the process of becoming one of the pillars of strength who finishes the journey regardless of the cost.

Focus Forward

I have loved my own journey (mostly) to date, but I'm excited that the new looks like walking on water.

This new season of life is about seeing broken humanity restored, and it is so alive in me that it is like the whole last season of life was simply preparation for the new. It feels strong and good.

In my heart of hearts, I have prayed over the years that the Lord himself would give me a revelation about what it means to serve the next generation, not just to be a leader or someone they can look up to, but rather someone to serve in their dreams, their visions, and their new ways of doing things. When I see people around me, half my age, carving out and pioneering their God-given pursuits, my heart is full, and I am continually challenged to keep dreaming and creating, not allowing my own processes to become stale and nostalgic.

But I am still me, and you are still you.

So let me ask you a question:

How are you doing with the whole deal of making room for others and handing over much of what used to be so you can walk into all that is before you?

One thing I do know is that when I hold on tightly to the old things, God cannot fill my hands with the new. Why not open your hands and lift them before God in worship? When you open them to loosen your grip on the "old," God can always be trusted to fill your heart and hands with something new that will continue to bring Him all the glory.

I'm not saying it will be easy, but I can guarantee it will not be

Loving conversations are not the result of forcing our opinions on others but rather of dying to self and preferring others.

as difficult as you think. John Maxwell said in a recent conversation with me, "If your most current topic is yesterday, then you're in trouble." Mmmm. Let's Selah on that. . . .

"LIFE AFFORDS NO GREATER RESPONSIBILITY, NO GREATER PRIVILEGE, THAN THE RAISING OF THE NEXT GENERATION."

C. Everett Koop

VALUE TWELVE:
PEOPLE

*God makes everything come out right; he puts victims back on
their feet. . . . God's love, though, is ever and always, eternally
present to all who fear him, making everything right for them and
their children as they follow his Covenant ways and remember
to do whatever he said.*

—Psalm 103:6, 18
The Message

One of the great quotes from my grandfather goes like
this: "As I look back over my life, and all the twists and
turns, the unexpected—the good and the bad—I can now
see the hand of God in it all." Talk about perspective. (Yes,
these are the same grandparents who sent Mark and me
a card on our twentieth wedding anniversary that read:
"Congratulations . . . and don't worry, the first twenty are
the worst!" Hmmm. More perspective.)

Learning to trust God through all the twists and turns of
life is indeed a strength that grows as you go with God. And
my heart in this chapter is to remind you that God is a lover

of people. His whole focus and attention is on people—and not just other people, but *you*. I've included *people* as a value because as one of God's people, I want to focus on your worth, not just the worth of those you lead or mentor. Essentially, this book was written to give you a few extra tools to assist in the transition period that occurs in helping people to rise up and take their place. But without actually sensing your own strong future forward, you could end up feeling displaced. And that is not God's intention for you.

Open Doors Await You

From the many conversations I've had with leaders in transition, I've found that letting go of the past can be very difficult, especially when you have regrets or when you're not sure about what is ahead. Whether we are hanging on to the past because of fear or failure, God has answers for us in the Word.

You've probably read Jeremiah 29:11 hundreds of times: " 'For I know the plans I have for you,' declares the LORD, 'plans to prosper you and not to harm you, plans to give you hope and a future.' " This is a promise. God is already in your next season, holding open the door and waiting for you to arrive. You might not know where you are headed, but He does—and that's where you have to keep your focus.

Philippians 3:13 encourages us to focus all our energies on what lies ahead rather than staying stuck and allowing ourselves to be emotionally tortured by what is in the past. It's been said that failure is like fertilizer; it stinks right now, but it will make you bloom bigger in the future.

The prophet Samuel learned this lesson. He had been the one to anoint Saul and establish him as king over God's people. He loved King Saul and was there at every turn to strengthen, encourage, and mentor him. However, when Saul disobeyed God and was rejected by God for his lack of commitment and love for the Lord, Samuel was sent to prophesy that the kingdom would be given to one better than he. Samuel was brokenhearted. He had invested so much of his time, effort, and care in his season of discipling Saul that he could not get beyond the grief. He was stuck in the past, full of regret.

But God had already stepped into Samuel's future, so He asked, "How long will you mourn for Saul, since I have rejected him as king over Israel? Fill your horn with oil and be on your way; I am sending you to Jesse of Bethlehem. I have chosen one of his sons to be king" (1 Samuel 16:1).

God is already in your next season, holding open the door and waiting for you to arrive.

And now we hear some of Samuel's excuses for not going forward:

> But Samuel said, "How can I go? If Saul hears about it, he will kill me." The Lord said, "Take a heifer with you and say, 'I have come to sacrifice to the Lord'" (v. 2).

Notice that God did not even respond to Samuel's fear of being killed by Saul. God wasn't concerned that the past threatened Samuel; He wanted Samuel to gain new perspective. He simply told him to go, and told him what to say and do when he got there. Samuel ignored his fear and just kept on obeying God, because that's what faith does.

Walk Your Faith Talk

Faith is the language God responds to when the future is foggy and you know it's impossible to go back. So let's talk about some ways you can improve your faith talk and get prepared for your next season.

I suggest you start by applying to yourself all the values that we've discussed in previous chapters—caring for your soul, dreaming, writing down your thoughts—especially encouraging yourself in the Lord. God himself has established you in himself, by His power and grace.

Romans 16:25-26 says, "Now to him who is able to establish you in accordance with my gospel, the message I proclaim about Jesus Christ, in keeping with the revelation of the mystery hidden for long ages past, but now revealed and made known through the prophetic writings by the command of the eternal God, so that all the Gentiles might come to the obedience that comes from faith." The Lord is guaranteeing His Word over your life by His name, and His covenant. Your future is established. God is on your side, making a way.

But a way to where? It's when we get caught in a web of questions that we start drifting into negative thinking. We forget that God is all about people—and not just other people; He is also for you.

During my own season of transition, I sat down with Isaiah 61 and read that prophecy over my life, out loud. I spoke it over my influence and my time, over the unspoken imaginings within my heart, asking God to speak with me, to walk with me, and to give me His perspective on this Scripture for my life.

I took out a new notebook, clean with potential, and prayed and wrote. The fact that I was in transition wasn't a mystery, but walking it out well *and* with purpose for the future was a mystery yet to be revealed. So I started sharing my questions with other people, and though the answers were well meaning, they were all very different. They were people's opinions, not God's, so they lacked His all-knowing perspective. That experience taught me that to shepherd other people well through transition and beyond, I had to hear from God myself, to really listen, and then follow His voice. And He spoke to me through Isaiah 61.

Direction in Distress

God is all about people. So Isaiah 61—"The Spirit of the Sovereign Lord is on me" chapter—is all about people. It's about how the Lord will use Jesus through you and me to bring freedom to people held in bondage, and to announce freedom to prisoners, and to comfort all who mourn, and the list goes on. The Spirit of the Lord has anointed you and me for this task, for this season. We are enabled, equipped, covered with His ability, and anointed for the task at hand. We are anointed to preach the Good News. He has sent us to the brokenhearted, to bring light into the darkness, to comfort the grief-stricken, to provide for the poor, to bestow crowns of beauty on those who feel ugly—to bring gladness and praise with us that unashamedly display the Lord's splendor. It says we will rebuild ancient ruins and restore ruined cities, and that finally righteousness and praise will spring up before all nations.

If what is before you appears bleak, woeful, or simply unclear, read this chapter of Scripture. Ask God to fill the chambers of your heart with renewed vigor for His purpose in the lives of people who are waiting for you in your next season. The first day I put pen to paper, I scrawled out pages and pages of thoughts. Then I started meditating and praying about them, asking the Lord to make known to me the things that would most delight His heart and impact people for His kingdom.

So let me get very vulnerable and give you a peek into what I call my "because" list. Some of what ended up on it looked like this: The Spirit of the Lord is upon me *because* . . .

- I have a complete conviction about my marriage and what it means to me, to my family, and to the generations to come. This conviction crafts my choices. I will not compromise. Mark and I are in this God-journey together, and our marriage will ebb and flow only to the tune of the "because" factor in our lives.

- I have a complete conviction about raising our daughters . . . and again, this will shape my decisions, keep me from compromising, and help me to live a life that is worthy of following. I will lead them to the Lord and His will for their lives.

- I have a complete conviction about the local church and the worship of God . . . that truth and creativity would resound from the earth in praise to Him . . . that I will serve in the house of God all the days of my life. I will not be distracted by good things but be captured by His presence, and His presence will define my life—not great opportunities or the praises of people.

- I have a complete conviction about bringing solutions to the many innocent people around the earth who are starving, downtrodden, and poor, to the many orphans and widows who are caught in wars and the aftermath of wars, natural disasters, and situations beyond their control. Fill my hands with answers, Lord, and fill my life with influence to bring change—that I would be found trustworthy!

- I have a complete conviction about raising and releasing the next generation—my role within the framework of leadership will be committed to seeing others fly! A new day for the body of Christ!

OK, I'll leave it there. The rest of my list is more personal, but perhaps this little glimpse will motivate you to spend some precious time alone with the Lord so you can start your own list. It will so help you to set your sights on things ahead and help you to stay sharp and focused. I find that when the winds of doubt and adversity begin to blow, I can regain stability and reset my sails by confidently going back to my "because" list and speaking the Word of Life over the atmosphere in my own heart.

He also has your course charted, so when you start to feel weary, remind yourself that you are anointed for the task at hand. Start to worship and pray, and fuel your love for Jesus. You are the hands He works through on earth. So remember, if your heart is not full, your hands will get tired.

Selah.

The gospel is all about people . . . God loving us, His children . . .

His children finding and loving Him . . .

and His children loving each other.

"Our lives should be a Hallelujah from head to toe."[1]

Augustine

VALUE **THIRTEEN:**
GENIUS

Not that I have already obtained all this, or have already arrived at my goal, but I press on to take hold of that for which Christ Jesus took hold of me.
—*Philippians 3:12*

Genius is everywhere. So we must ask ourselves, Do I recognize it? And are we secure enough to release it in those we mentor? Columnist Gene Weingarten of *The Washington Post* wondered if genius could be recognized in a commonplace setting that was not prepared to receive it. So on January 12, 2007, amidst the morning rush, he convinced Joshua Bell—one of the world's leading violinists—to perform a solo concert at the entrance to L'Enfant metro station in Washington, DC. Dressed in jeans, a long-sleeved T-shirt, and a baseball cap, Bell diverted attention from his true identity. Instead of a tin cup, he placed a violin case on the ground and dropped in a few dollars for seed. He then picked up his $3.5 million Stradivarius and began to play. And would you believe that within a quarter hour, hidden cameras filmed more than a thousand people who rushed by without pause to listen to the musical genius—a man whose talents can command $1,000 a minute![1]

Joshua's musical talents revealed themselves at a young age. When he was four, his mother noticed that he had collected rubber bands and stretched them across the handles on his dresser drawers to imitate the music his mother played on the piano. His mother and father enrolled him in violin lessons and invested in a handmade violin, one customized to his small size. His parents, both practicing psychologists, recognized his genius and released him into it.

Open Your Eyes to His Genius

The chances of genius in your midst are very high. I've sat in rehearsals and listened to some of the new songs being written by these younger men and women and left the building in shock at the brilliance! When I read the scripts they're writing, feast my eyes on the artwork they're creating, and catch a glimpse of the fashions they're constructing, I am inspired!

Look around you—genius is everywhere just waiting for its appointed time.

Romans 1:20 says, "For since the creation of the world God's invisible qualities—his eternal power and divine nature—have been clearly seen, being understood from what has been made, so that people are without excuse." God's invisible qualities, His genius, can be clearly seen, but we have to stop long enough to look, listen, and linger with those whom God has placed in our path.

I see genius in people all around me. I see it as a true reflection of the creative nature of our God, even when He remains unacknowledged. I see it in architecture, I hear it in music, I feel it during a movie that unravels my emotions, I taste it when eating delectable foods and I touch it when handling exquisite fabrics and surfaces.

But when I see genius in the house of God—people using their gifts to express devotion—I can hardly stand it, because it is so good!

Sadly, I have also seen many genius types drift in and out of church, wondering whether they have anything to contribute. Some are overlooked simply because they approach their creativity in ways that counter the status quo and bring more intensity than we have known.

With genius in our midst, we must learn to get out of the way, to listen to the intensity of thought, and to encourage the passion with definitive intent. And we must make way for allowing the process of achieving the outcome to be different from the methods we have used in the past. It's hard to do, let me tell you, especially when you can see a smarter way to achieve the outcome. But you and I must learn that there are many ways to achieve a great creative result. I have discovered that different is often just that—different—not worse or greater, just different.

Get good at loving the different.

As leaders, we must become equipped to inspire the greatly talented in our midst. So if you have trouble doing that, think back to the time when you sensed God leading you to the place where you are today, to the time when His gentle but persuasive voice echoed deep in the chambers of your heart. You didn't do things exactly the way others did them, but when God *Look* and man spoke hope into your potential, you *around* felt safe enough to explore your "different." *you—genius* Now it's your privilege to reconcile people's *is everywhere* hearts with the Father so they too feel safe *just waiting for* enough to release the genius within— *its appointed time.* the different He put in each one of us.

Applaud the "Different" in Others

Moses recognized the different in Joshua. Moses knew he had taken the people as far as they could go under his leadership. He had the vision for the Promised Land, but Joshua's genius—his "different"—would be needed to cross over and conquer the new territory. Moses shepherded the people *through* the wilderness; Joshua would take them *into* the Promised Land and help them to possess it.

Elijah recognized the different in Elisha. God Almighty used Elijah to confront those who worshiped false gods; he wrought miracles of judgment to establish God's truth and power. Elijah was the groundbreaker, the way-maker for Elisha. So when Elisha asked for a double portion of Elijah's mantle, the spiritual ground had already been prepared to bring in the next level of miracles, those of mercy and grace.

Many leaders today are so intimidated by the Joshua and Elisha in their midst that they fail to remember who it was that stood on the mountain with Jesus when He was transfigured— none other than Moses and Elijah (see Matthew 17). God does not forget the ones who establish, even when their successors have had a double portion of victory. He gives one the genius to imagine and break ground; He gives another the genius to complete the vision and set it up for their successors.

Each one of us has a part in the eternal story that God is writing. And whenever I sense insecurity over my own small part to play, I think back on some of those moments when heaven intervened to change my life's course, when the heart of God resonated with mine, putting my feet on solid ground and establishing my way. It doesn't take long for the insecurities to start melting away in the light of His truth and glory. The historical heroes got it right. They didn't see their small piece in the divine jigsaw puzzle of life as being minimized. They kept their focus on God, and realized that their moment in history was only a part of the greater story. And we need to remember that too!

Hebrews 12:1-2 says it all: "Therefore we also, since we are surrounded by so great a cloud of witnesses, let us lay aside very weight, and the sin which so easily ensnares us, and let us run with endurance the race that is set before us, looking unto Jesus, the author and finisher of our faith, who for the joy that was set before Him endured the cross, despising the shame, and has sat down at the right hand of the throne of God" (NKJV).

Transitioning the Undone

I love the story about Walt Disney, who planned and dreamed Disneyland and didn't even live to see it become what it is today—yet I think he did see it. He saw it in his mind, in his heart, and in every fingerprint that influenced the final outcome. He talked about it, drew plans consistently, made plans for its eventuality, but his very positive legacy of the undone meant that what was in his heart would be completed and taken to the next level by others.

We see this same transitioning from dream planner to dream builder with King David and Solomon. David had it in his heart to build a house in which to rest the ark of the covenant. But God said David was not to build it; He had chosen David's son to complete the work. David was not embittered or resentful that God had chosen Solomon. He accepted God's decision and encouraged Solomon: "Be strong and courageous, and do the work. Do *not* be afraid or discouraged, for the Lord God, my God, is with you" (1 Chronicles 28:20, emphasis added). I love that. David gives Solomon the how-to's and, more important, encourages Solomon to trust God, to seek God, and to do the work.

Check out 1 Chronicles 28:9-10. It says, "And you, my son Solomon, acknowledge the God of your father, and serve him with wholehearted devotion and with a willing mind, for the

Lord searches every heart and understands every desire and every thought. If you seek him, he will be found by you; but if you forsake him, he will reject you forever. Consider now, for the Lord has chosen you to build a house as the sanctuary. Be strong and *do the work"* (emphasis added).

I like what Thomas Edison said: "Genius is 1 percent inspiration and 99 percent perspiration." Someone can have a mother lode of genius and never use it. Therefore, like David, we need to encourage those we mentor to stay true to God, to keep their hearts pure, and to do the work of developing their genius.

And in the process, we leaders must also stay true to God, keep our hearts pure, and do the work of building up people for God's purposes.

I wonder how you or I would respond if God told us that we were to hand off the things we most wanted to accomplish. I wonder how we would respond to hearing that our successors would not only take our plans to the next level but also bring some sort of genius to the mix that would make the vision even greater in their season of history.

David's stunning prayer in 1 Chronicles 29 brings the story of his own transfer of leadership to a climax of thanksgiving. It's all about the heart. Can God trust your heart enough to mentor genius?

Discipling Genius

Here's the thing about genius and the greatly gifted: What they bring is usually so easy for them that they cannot explain how they do it—because it is a gift! Their gift has made a way for them, and we can all become so blinded by the gift that we forget about character. Some people have genius in one area, but no maturity in another. Discipling of genius can present quite a challenge.

For me, the pastoring of genius—walking people through

success, through creative disappointments, and waiting for character to catch up with the gifting—has been one of the greatest challenges to date. I hear leaders say that all their problems would be solved if they only had more "well-known, crazily talented people" on their team. But I wonder if they are secure enough, and confident enough, to pastor and challenge the areas of their lives that would need to be confronted.

I've heard stories told and retold about the difficulty in convincing the sports genius, musical genius—any kind of genius—to become a part of the church community. The problem is not just that the genius thinks he or she can play by a different set of principles. No, the problem can, and usually does, trickle down from flaws in leadership—leaders being intimidated, being infatuated, or using the giftedness to bolster their own position among their peers. I know I am making a blanket statement, but to be honest, I have seen this happen so many times that the exception is truly the exception.

So we end up with genius being all around us, yet needing leaders who are grounded and large-hearted enough to simply let the brilliance shine while still encouraging strong disciplines, such as making the Word of God a priority and building strong church and family life. Another priority in mentoring genius is guiding them through success if it comes, and sticking with them if it doesn't. If you will not disciple them, how can God trust you with the privilege of making them a part of your team? It would be wonderful if the exceptionally gifted in your community knew they could come to you for the finest godly counsel because you care more about their godliness than your own desire for recognition. That kind of leadership will ignite the complacent.

Get Your Heart Right

Leaders, we are all part of this amazing race, running in our own lanes, but running with a baton to pass on beautifully to the next runner. In my relay, I want the baton that I hand to my next runner in this "life relay" to be a hot, on-fire baton—a baton that represents miracles, a baton that represents a journey carved out in faith, filled with creative expression, and abundant with continued hope and expectation. I do not want to hand over a baton that is tired, worn out, disillusioned, and resentful.

Today I plucked up some tiny weeds that were sprouting in my garden, only to find that huge thorns had already developed on them in their tiny state! I was reminded that God asks us to remain committed to keeping our hearts pure so that no weeds of offense, jealousy, or pride have opportunity to grow roots or prickles.

C'mon leader, stand tall, speak with grace and courage, release others, and trust God with your own life.

When genius comes into your midst, it is absurd to think there is not room for all of you or that your part of the journey will be minimized by those who are called to a grander scale. Encourage the different in others; don't try to control it. Our God is the God of addition and multiplication—so let Him multiply your mantle through others.

All Things Are Possible

I clearly recall the day Australians heard the news that our nation would have the privilege of hosting the Olympic Games in the city of Sydney. We were all so excited, and the excitement gained even more momentum as plans for constructing stadiums and huge sporting venues were aired through various media outlets. I sensed straightaway that these stadiums would eventually be used for the glory of our God, and that there would even be a day when they would be too small. It still amazes me to think that we can take a worship event into a stadium. Each time I stand there, I get a buzz wondering how on earth this happened. And the heart of the church is also encouraged to know that the Spirit of the Lord is moving in such a powerful way—that His church is alive and well.

Encourage the different in others; don't try to control it.

But you know, for our children, this magnitude is so normal. They talk about filling all the gigantic football stadiums, not just the stadiums of thirty and forty thousand. No, what was crazy great for us is just their beginning, and it's here that we see Ephesians 3:20 coming into play—"immeasurably more than all we ask or imagine" . . . such is the nature of our God.

Pretty amazing, hey?

Revelation 15:3–4 reveals this song of the overcomers, and I pray you hear it as a great testimony to all that God has done, is doing, and is going to do:

"Great and marvelous are your deeds, Lord God Almighty. Just and true are your ways, King of the nations. Who will not fear you, O Lord, and bring glory to your name? For you alone are holy. All nations will come and worship before you, for your righteous acts have been revealed."

Look around you . . . His genius is everywhere!

"There's a genius in all of us."

Albert Einstein

VALUE FOURTEEN:
HEARTS OF FLESH

He has showed you, O mortal, what is good. And what does the
LORD *require of you? To act justly and to love mercy and to walk*
humbly with your God.

—Micah 6:8

The great love of God fuels our being. The Great Commission fuels our doing.

Remember the day you said yes to Jesus? Remember how He turned your stony heart into one that was undivided, a heart so grateful that you would have done anything and helped everyone just to please the heart of God? Ezekiel 11:19 says, "I will give them an undivided heart and put a new spirit in them; I will remove from them their heart of stone and give them a heart of flesh." And that's how we *all* start out.

That is . . . until life happens. Then we get overloaded with the concerns of doing life and facing its challenges, hurts, and hurdles, until suddenly God slips into second place. Slowly and subtly our hearts of flesh start to harden, and the doing fuels our being until our commission becomes more important than our love for God. Eventually we become stonyhearted human doers instead of softhearted human beings whose lives are set apart for God. A stony heart, like stony ground, gives out but it doesn't absorb. And the heart once changed by the love of God finds life in a Christian bubble that remains untouched by the things that have touched His heart.

Hearts of stone are often hearts that have been wounded, overburdened, and disappointed. The walls of the heart have toughened to prevent the absorption of more pain and to preserve the appearance of life. Left un-dealt with, these hearts can become cynical, untrusting, and able to see dire need and feel nothing. They can even live in continual violence and be seemingly unaffected.

I have seen kids, having lost their entire family through genocide in Rwanda, who have to fend for themselves on the streets until either someone comes to help, or death comes and brings relief. And because death is the expected lot in their lives, their beautiful little hearts become hardened to hope so they can cope with tomorrow's trouble, if tomorrow comes at all.

What a tragedy. Yet we have the absolute antidote to hardness of heart, which is simply found in seeking first the kingdom of God so that His love can pour through us with service to others.

Hearts Fully Alive

Nothing arrests a complacent or inactive heart more than meeting needs head on and living to lift the lives of others. A heart alive in Christ sees need and has to do something about it. A heart alive in Christ is soft, sensitive, and obedient to the voice of the Holy Spirit. A heart fully alive is dangerous to the kingdom of darkness.

A heart fully alive recognizes seasonal shifts and prepares well for the changes. It readies itself for fueling others who are willing to receive life. It is open and communicative, not self-protective or manipulative. A heart fully alive is honored to host the presence of God and fulfill His every desire.

This chapter's opening verse, Micah 6:8, asks the question: So .what is it that the Lord *really* desires from you? More sacrifices? More public displays of your devotion?

The answer is strong and straight to the point: "To act justly and to love mercy and to walk humbly with your God."

To "act justly" is to do the right thing before God no matter what the cost to self. To "love mercy" is to refuse to judge others. James 2:13 says, "Mercy triumphs over judgment." Mercy loves no matter what the sacrifice, and responds to human pain. And to "walk humbly with your God" simply means that you walk dependent upon His voice—living a life that is "set apart" to care for the things that are important to Him.

So when it gets down to the call and purposes of God for each of our lives, the state of our heart is critical to the whole story. For without His power at work in our hearts, we easily become unaware of the need all around us, or within us, so that we either go through the motions of Christianity or become slaves to a works-based theology—which may fool others but doesn't impress God.

Working for love instead of from love is the result of making self the God of your heart. When self is exalted, you live to please others, and your actions are driven by your need to get approval from those around you—rather than being fueled by a heart overflowing with love for God and a conviction to serve Christ regardless of the price. This is a lesson that every one of us must learn somewhere along life's journey. *Working for love instead of from love is the result of making self the God of your heart.*

God's Burden Bearers

One trait I love about the generations coming up is that they don't want to invest their time in worthless efforts. And I love what we're seeing in churches around the globe: There is an intensity and increased passion to see mission endeavors result in changed lives. This effort to help the hurting is spreading like wildfire, often being led by young, radical Christians who have made it their goal to live out Micah 6:8.

One of our dear friends is a young man named Hugh Evans, the founder of a great charity called the Oaktree Foundation. It's an aid and development organization run entirely by young volunteers who are committed to empowering developing communities through education in a way that is sustainable.

Hugh's goal was to hand over the leadership of Oaktree by the time he turned twenty-six. And he did. Remarkable! What's even more impressive is that every volunteer is also under the age of twenty-six. We have attended some of their functions, and the passion and ability to accomplish their goals is amazing.

And this is the cry of young people everywhere: they want to be involved in something greater than themselves; they want to be involved in something that helps to relieve human suffering, locally and globally.

Paul O'Rourke, the CEO of Compassion Australia, writes in the book *Blessings of the Poor*:

> The poor who know Jesus are wonderful ambassadors for what is valuable in God's Kingdom. They trust in Jesus because they must; their very existence depends on His provision. They are unencumbered by the world's deceptive trappings of pride, envy, and self-sufficiency. They work hard, are thankful for what they have, and focus on the things that are important: faith, family and friends.
>
> The poor have taught me many things, including humility, dignity, the sacrifice of worship, faith, hope, joy,

generosity and contentment. I have discovered that you can't out-give either God or the poor.[1]

Paul reminds us that even as God's heart is revealed through our willingness to bring relief and answers to the developing world, so we also have much to learn from those who are suffering. Character is forged more purely in the fire than in the fun times.

It is essential, therefore, that when we mentor the younger generations, we help them to see what is happening in these desperately needy nations. And there are many ways to heighten their awareness of those less fortunate. Get them involved in giving to mission programs, send teams overseas to work in the field, hook up with trusted ministries, sponsor children through connect groups or friendship circles, and teach them always to pray for those who are suffering and persecuted. In the end, we present opportunities for them to participate in, and then simply continue to teach the importance of not only talking about needs but also committing to bring resolve by doing the work.

When we help others, we worship God. The key is to keep the focus on the heart of God so that our work comes from the overflow of our love for Him.

Character is forged more purely in the fire than in the fun times.

The Glory Belongs to God

Our God is the ultimate Father. He never violates our freedom to choose, especially when it comes to worship. He does not need our worship, we do. It's in worship that we are found by Him (see John 4:23). And it is when we get real and vulnerable in the presence of the Almighty that He brings about change in our hearts.

For years I wrestled with the uneasy question in my spirit— what is the change for? And I finally felt inspired with a simple

Holy Spirit answer: Our change is for people. All of our worship belongs to God; all glory belongs to God—and He uses our lives, as they slowly change and mirror Him, to take His love in varied forms to people all over this planet. Anyone in leadership must learn this.

One reason many artists—world famous "musos" and singers, actors, etc.—have trouble coping in the spotlight is that our human bodies were not designed for glory. We were never designed to receive it, only to give it to the One who breathed life into us. When you or I receive glory, and keep on receiving it, eventually it will destroy our souls.

The glory belongs to God, but His passion is not to receive glory. He's certainly not sitting in heaven going, "Yes, more glory for me, more glory for me." No! A thousand times no!

His passion is you.

His passion is me.

His passion is our neighbors, our families, the homeless kids sleeping on the streets, the prostitutes who are trying to make a living to feed their drug habit in order to silence the raging pain within.

Our God is passionate about people.

Practice Heaven on Earth

Jesus washed the feet of His disciples. He served people so they might become good receivers and then use what they have received to serve others. I often use the foot-washing illustration because it clearly demonstrates the way worship works. When leading people in worship, metaphorically we come washing their feet, taking their troubled souls and pointing them to Christ through the restful fragrance of our own truthful worship.

When Jesus sits at the well with the broken woman in John 4, He is far more interested in healing the woman's broken heart than protecting His own reputation, or hers. She is a Samaritan, a group that is disrespected and forsaken by Jews. She is also a woman, and rabbis never spoke to women in public. But she is thirsty, and the life she's been drinking in has not satisfied her soul. So Jesus offers the living water that is available to her by drinking in His life—water that has the power to sustain her throughout all of her years, water that cleanses the heart and washes it from the inside out. And this "God encounter" causes her to abandon her waterpot to run and tell others. One word from Jesus and the things that once mattered are suddenly abandoned.

The economy of heaven is people. And when we depart from this earthly life, we can't take anything with us but those who have sipped from our cup of living water.

The Word says, "Thy kingdom come, Thy will be done in earth, as it is in heaven" (Matthew 6:10 KJV), so the value is people, but the atmosphere is worship. Revelation 14:2–3 gives a sneak preview into the sound of heaven—extreme worship for sure! And my creative juices get going as I envision and hear this scene being played out like a Spielberg special-effects showcase:

"And I heard a sound from heaven like the roar of rushing waters and like a loud peal of thunder. The sound I heard was like that of harpists playing their harps. And they sang a new song before the throne and before the four living creatures and the elders. No one could learn the song except the 144,000 who had been redeemed from the earth."

I love it . . . the sound of praise like the rushing of mighty waters. Revelation 5:13 says, "To him who sits on the throne and to the Lamb be praise and honor and glory and power, for ever and ever"—that's the sound of heaven, and we get to practice it here on earth.

But what is the sound of the earth? It's a groaning, a weeping— a hollow and hopeless sound, a sound of torment from those who are broken, enslaved, and afflicted. It's the sound that implored the heart of God to send Jesus.

There's a big gap, my friend, a great divide between the sound of heaven and the sound of earth that seems impossible to breach. But it's right there in that gap that we discover our role as the bride of Christ. We are the nurturers, the overcomers, the hands and feet of Jesus sent to bridge the gap, generation to generation, the redeemed to the unredeemed. We are the bridge-builders who lead people from darkness to light, from hopelessness to abundant joy, from bondage to freedom.

Our lives have been raised up to tear down the walls of injustice and see the dawn break over our earth. And we leaders need to inspire others to be the change that the world needs.

Your Life Is Your Worship

I am so passionate about helping those on our team to see that worship is not to be clothed in a performance to parade before men; it's getting raw and real before the Lord. Our God is not looking for perfection in our gifting; He's looking for authenticity in our hearts. Only in a heart that beats for God can we find real compassion, the emotional stop sign that Jesus most often responded to.

The story of the Good Samaritan is another of my favorites because the Good Samaritan lifted the life of another. When he saw a man bloodied, beaten, and lying on the side of the road, he secured his broken heart with care, he secured his broken body with a place to recover, and he secured his total healing with provision for the future. He saw the need, responded with kindness, and followed through until the man was restored. The Good Samaritan built margin into his day

The economy of heaven is people.

to help people, while others simply rushed past. A heart set apart for God *cannot* overlook injustice.

To be known as a Christian leader and not be known for the love in your heart is an absolute travesty—but one that can be remedied through His power at work in us. We don't want to be just singers of songs but also lovers of God. We want to be tenderhearted lovers who use the whole of our lives, our Romans 12 understanding of worship, to say:

"Hey, this injustice stops with me."

When God is alive in our hearts, everything we say and do is worship. When we relieve human suffering, we worship Him. When we renounce our right to be right, we worship Him. When we follow His leading, no matter the cost to self, we worship Him. Our worship is simply this—to act justly and to love mercy and to walk humbly with our God. And when we do . . .

The great love of God fuels our being . . .

The Great Commission fuels our doing.

YOU HAVE SHOWN US
Words and Music by CompassionArt

VERSE 1:
You have shown us, O God,
What is good
You have shown us, O Lord,
What You require
You have heard all our songs
How we long to worship
You've taught us
The offering You desire

CHORUS:
To do justly
(and) To love mercy
(and) To walk humbly with You, God

VERSE 2:
You have shown us
The riches of Your love
You have shown us
Your heart for those in need
You have opened our ears
To the cries of the poor
You have called us
To be Your hands and feet

BRIDGE:
To the oppressed and the broken
To the widow and the orphan
Let the river of Your justice
Flow through us

"HOW WONDERFUL IT IS THAT NOBODY NEED WAIT A **SINGLE MINUTE** BEFORE **STARTING** TO **IMPROVE** THE WORLD."[2]

Anne Frank

FINALE:
A STUDY OF DEVOTION

A Worship Overview for
Meditation and for Teaching

Devotion: committed love, dedication, enthusiasm, religious fervor, the act of devoting; fervent love and loyalty expressed through service, sacrifice, and submission.

Devotion is a beautiful word. It rolls off the tongue and actually carries with it the sounds of its meaning. But devotion is not just a word that pleases the senses, it is a word that demands more than a physical or cognitive response, indeed it requires the whole of your being, including *all* of your heart and soul.

Devotion is born out of revelation—God revealing to our hearts His love and devotion toward us so that we can in turn reveal our hearts of love and devotion to Him. Devotion is the reciprocity of the heart. It is responding to a divine transaction that happens deep within, requiring us to dig deeper, to give more of self, to give all of our energy and focus to Him. It is an attitude of a single-minded heart that says, "He is first. I will magnify Him above all else." It's surrendering feelings, thoughts, and emotions to Him.

And it's the word *devotion* that I will apply to our journey of worship, because this word describes most clearly the heart voyage that is part of understanding the wholehearted commitment of loving, serving, and following Christ.

Worship cannot be confined to music, or fully played, or described by the psalmist, although these are all part of our desire to express love to God in song. However, when we sing, we find that Martin Luther was right in saying, "He who sings prays twice."

More than forty psalms ask us to sing unto our God, for He can never be praised enough. But let me talk you through a brief biblical overview of worship—its intent, its origin, and its purpose.

A Response to His Love

The exhausting thought for me is that although God himself is complete without us, He still chooses to be *incomplete* without us. His love for us is so deep, so endless, so all encompassing that even though He has the universe at His feet, our expressions of love for Him are what delight His heart the most. He knows all about us—our names, the color of our eyes, the number of hairs on our head, our gifts, our talents, our hopes, and our failings . . . every little secret desire and hurt within our hearts. Yes, our God cares for His kids, and He inhabits our praises with the fullness of himself.

Worship is born out of the revelation of God's love for us; it is a response to God's initiative. First John 4:19 says, "We love him, because *he first loved us*" (KJV, emphasis added).

Before we knew Him, He loved us. Before we called Him Lord,

He called us His. Nothing—no height, nor depth—can compare to the great love of God. And with that love in mind, we worship. And our worship is not only in deed but also in song—to sing the song of the redeemed, the song of our hearts, joining the manifesto of song that spans from the beginning of time until now. It is the song of the sons and daughters of God trying to express something of the magnitude and the wonder of His saving grace.

An Eternal Song

The worship of God is timeless and eternal—spanning from when Adam and Eve and their family at the end of Genesis 4 lean in closer to God in thanksgiving for remembering them, through to when the morning stars join in on the choruses in Job 38 and beyond. King David displays his care about worship in 1 Chronicles when he puts together the huge choir and orchestra for the tabernacle worship. Mary is found singing the "Magnificat" in Luke 1, and Jesus sings a hymn of praise with the disciples in Matthew 26.

The song of God has continued throughout history—man pouring out of the deep places in his heart, reaching out to a God who sent His precious son Jesus Christ, who through the resurrection power of the cross displayed a love so great that separation from God was given solution, and the veil that once separated us from His presence was torn from top to bottom, making a way for us to know Him on every level. First Peter 1:6–9 says:

> I know how great this makes you feel, even though you have to put up with every kind of aggravation in the meantime. Pure gold put in the fire comes out of it proved pure; genuine faith put through this suffering comes out proved genuine. When Jesus wraps this all up, it's your faith, not your gold, that God will have on display as evidence of his victory. You never saw him, yet you love him. You still

179

don't see him, yet you trust him—with laughter and singing. Because you kept on believing, you'll get what you're looking forward to: total salvation (THE MESSAGE).

What we are part of today has been building for generations: truthful worship produced through persecution and pain, refined as pure gold; and the song goes on. It's the song of faith, not our gifts or abilities, but the sound of the Spirit of God alive within us that makes the song, the stance, and the mystery alive! And as He is pursued and welcomed among us, the felt evidence of the Holy Spirit in our midst continues to build momentum, calling the lost home and stoking the embers of hearts that have become lukewarm.

His Spirit Touching Ours

The significance of His glory and His presence is of eternal and immeasurable weight. From age to age, everlasting to everlasting, when His Spirit touches ours, there is worship. Here's how Richard Foster describes it:

> Worship is our responding to the overtures of love from the heart of the Father. Its central reality is found "in Spirit and in Truth." It is kindled within us only when the Spirit of God touches our human spirit. Forms and rituals do not produce worship, nor does the formal disuse of forms and rituals. We can use all the right techniques and methods, we can have the best possible liturgy (a form and arrangement of public worship laid down by a church or religion), but we have not worshiped the Lord until Spirit touches spirit . . . singing, praying, praising, all may lead to worship, but worship is more than any of them. Our spirit must be ignited by divine fire.[1]

True worship is revealed when we declare God's worth— *weorthscipe*, which in essence means "ascribed worth." Worthship!

It is *not* an expression of devotion that can be fully grasped or contained by the mind, even though this truth frustrates many believers who would feel safer if it were. It is an expression released through the heart, inasmuch as our language of thanksgiving and adoration are given voice via this gateway of love.

Worship Starts With Living Loved

Psalm 18 paints a vivid picture of how God's heart is moved by the plight and ache of humanity and how His love for you and me fuels His motivation for everything He does. Thus, without some sort of understanding of God's love for you, it is difficult to express a genuine thank-you. So rather than trying, trying, trying to love Him more, the key is to simply meditate on His great love for you. Before long, you'll sense a new understanding of what it actually means to "enter into His gates with thanksgiving."

Most of us seem to struggle to receive a love that accepts us just as we are, that loves us beyond our faults, and loves us to life even though we don't deserve it. In this performance-based world, you can actually tie yourself up in knots trying to be "good enough" to worship. People often say, "I just don't deserve this great love. I don't deserve to have it poured out over my life." And it's true; we don't deserve it. It is God's longing to be with us that initiates and perpetuates His unconditional love for us and qualifies us for worship.

John 1:14 says: "The Word became flesh and dwelt among us" (NKJV). We did not earn or deserve His fellowship, but we are loved and have been made right with God through the blood of Jesus. God sees us and knows us intimately, yet still desires to be with us. I know that when I was first saved, I was all wrapped up in my own little very, very disheartened world. I didn't expect God to show up. I didn't behave perfectly or try to do good things with the hope that some higher power would accept me. No, God found me, and when He did, I found Him. The result was that my little world changed forever.

I still find it hard to fathom the power that lives in me, or why God chose me. But He did. He chose each one of us. He then filled our hearts with His presence and power, the same power that raised Christ from the dead. Go figure.

So grace stands guard over our hearts and protects us from ourselves, the "Trying too hard" generation. In being so desperate to get it right, we actually end up a very long way from where the simplicity of truth begs us to journey. None of us could ever be good enough, clever enough, right enough, or whole enough—and that's the point of our need for a Savior. And through His saving grace, our response in worship is a surprise, but the closest thing to heaven we'll experience here on earth.

Worship is a supernatural action, the response of the created to the Creator. Isaiah 43:6-7 says that we were all created for His glory—not for ours, for His.

Worship is a faith response, a response to distinct revelation. It carries many strands of devotion, from the most simple to the most sublime. The active life of a worshiper pours itself out in a sacrificial manner, starting in obedience, and finding itself in adoration and consecration. The worshiper finds himself or herself in the position of a servant, heart and hands ready to do the will of the Father. John 5:30 says, "I can do nothing on My own initiative. . . . I do not seek My own will, but the will of Him who sent Me" (NASB). Worship brings us to a place of surrendering our rights and choosing to give Him complete control of our lives.

It Begins and Ends With Him

Worship, at every level, begins and ends with God as the priority—God showing us the Father's heart of love for us, God counseling, comforting, and guiding us through the voice of the precious Holy Spirit, and God in the person of Jesus Christ who is our Mediator and Way-Maker into the throne room of heaven. We make it all about Him, and He turns it around and makes it all about us, His Spirit at work in and through us that we might say, "I am His, and He is mine."

Through worship, humanity enters into the spiritual universe that consists of the ceaseless proclamation of God's glory. Creation has always been poised, ready to delight the heart of God.

In worship, we are kept in constant remembrance of the unchanging, ever holy nature of God and His power to change us into His likeness.

Some of the biblical truths about the worship of God:

- We all worship (anthropologists agree about this fact).
- The gospel is a call to worship, to lay down our lives, and take up His cross.
- We worship in the Spirit of God and boast in Jesus Christ (Philippians 3:3).
- Worship involves the whole of our lives (Romans 12).
- Worship, when offered from the body of Christ, both gathered and scattered, is a continual reminder of our shared story and identity in Christ.
- Worship is the promised future of earth and heaven. Revelation 5:13 says, "Then I heard every creature in heaven and on earth and under the earth and in the sea. They sang: 'Blessing and honor and glory and power belong to the one sitting on the throne and to the Lamb forever and ever'" (NLT).
- Worship is so valuable that the battle for our worship is constant, ongoing. Satan tries to entice Jesus with cunning,

empty words when he says in Matthew 4, "Bow down and worship me." Jesus, of course, has the ultimate victory, but when you are vulnerable, be on the lookout. That's when the enemy comes to challenge your passion for God and offer you something else in exchange. In Isaiah 14, Satan says, "I will ascend into heaven. I will exalt my throne above the stars of God" (NKJV). It's the age-old story of pride.

• Worship identifies the kingdom that you belong to.

In the end, it's all about love—God's love first for us, and our response of love to Him. It's easy to sing about love, to share it, to talk about it, but to receive it freely is a major mindblower! It is love that causes the heart to trust Him in prayer, and the intimacy established in prayer causes the heart to respond in worship.

Spontaneous Prayer

There are no prayers like prayers offered in worship.

First Thessalonians 5:17–18 tells us: *"Be unceasing in prayer* [praying perseveringly]; *thank [God] in everything* [no matter what the circumstances may be, be thankful and give thanks], for this is the will of God for you [who are] in Christ Jesus" (AMP, emphasis added).

Revelation 5 describes a scene in heaven of elders holding a harp (depicting worship), and each of them also has golden bowls full of incense, which are the prayers of God's people. I love this scene of prayer and worship coming before God, songs being sung throughout heaven declaring His majesty and reign and the victory He has won over every need.

Some people pray loud and confident bold prayers—they give no thought to who may hear. Others offer their prayers in whispers and moments of total silence.

Many prayers are wrapped in music and melodies that allow

the one praying to be fully engaged when otherwise he or she might find it harder to enter the courts of God. Never underestimate the power of your prayers. Be committed to raising up a powerful team of warriors who pray the Word and sing with clarity and conviction.

I pray that a revelation of God's love is utmost in your heart and life, and with that revelation will come an increased burning desire to see others receive this revelation of love too. Worship kicks into a whole new level when we become truly convinced that we are loved. The result of our being loved is confidence in Christ and His power to shape our character, our language, our behavior, our songs, our time, our talents, and our passions.

God Sees the Love, Not the Method

Unfortunately, all of us are capable of turning our conviction about what it means to serve and worship Christ into our own personal latest theology so that we discount or judge others for serving and worshiping the Lord in ways that do not meet our expectations.

Methods, skill, atmosphere, tried-and-true techniques—none of these will ever take the place of a God-encounter . . . never can and never will! The truth is that the Word is full of challenge and encouragement to trust in the Lord with our whole heart, and the rest—the sounds, the style, the musical preferences, etc.—can and must morph and change as every generation brings a new song and a new fabric to the rich tapestry woven for generations in this kingdom realm.

As we near the end of this book, please remember to let your life be empowered and motivated by His great love for you and at work in you. Mother Teresa said, "It's not what you do, but how much love you put into it that counts."

As we lead and encourage all those who are coming after

us, remember that it is in loving that we are most like Christ, because . . . God is love.

Devotion is not only worship, music, giving, justice, songs, hymns, or choruses; it is responding to the love we have received with love that reaches upward for Him, outward for others, and inward for ourselves.

The Word says the whole law can be summed up in one command: Love others as you love yourself (see Matthew 7:12).

John 3:16 tells us: "For God *so loved* . . . that he gave" (emphasis added). Living loved is a powerful, God-breathed concept, and if we would get it, really get it—*wow*, that would be revolutionary!

A Legacy of Love

Love means legacy. Without love, we simply exist, and we cannot reproduce what we do not have within us. Worship without love is just music; relationships without love are simply acquaintances; congregations without love are just clubs; worship teams without love are just bands; songs without love are just jingles. Love is the ingredient that changes everything. A problem tackled without love ends in war; a pursuit of Christ without love ends in religion; wealth or inheritance gained without love ends in greed.

Love is the ingredient that changes everything.

Do you need change? Receive His love. Please know today how much you are loved. Even if you don't feel it, you cannot change the fact that you are, so live like you are. Let's live loved, lead loved, and serve loved—and with strength and grace, pass on all that we know to the next generation.

Let me finish with a story:

Many years ago, on my first trip to Rwanda, I walked back into our hotel after a long day out in the field. My heart was breaking and aching with frustration, not knowing how to do more but knowing I must. Word must have spread that we were staying at this particular hotel, because the room was filled with orphans who were now young adults, obviously Christians who loved to worship but had lived really tough lives. Children raising children.

The words echoed in the foyer: "Mumma, Mumma," and these kids huddled around me on all sides, touching, hugging, crying, "Mumma, you came." Somehow, the music of our church had come to them years before, bringing comfort and strength and a sense of security. In later conversations they shared how, when they were looking for a mum (or mom), I sang to them, and had sung them to sleep ever since, teaching the Word of God and speaking life over them.

I was humbled and challenged that day, and a sense of resolve settled deep within my spirit as I realized that every choice you and I make has a chance to influence the next generation one way or the other—either up close or from afar.

If I could stand in front of you now, I would sign off by saying how much I truly love and believe in you, and even more so, how much God himself loves and believes in you. With love received and love to give, let's handle this season of time that God has entrusted to us with grace and strength, and let's pass on all that we know to the next generation. Humanity is counting on it.

With all my heart,

God can do anything, you know—far more than you could ever imagine or guess or request in your wildest dreams! He does it not by pushing us around but by working within us, his Spirit deeply and gently within us. Glory to God in the church! Glory to God in the Messiah, in Jesus! Glory down all the generations! Glory through all millennia! Oh, yes!

—*Ephesians 3:20–21*
THE MESSAGE

THANK YOU . . .

To my husband, Mark, serving God together forever, what a ride, babe! I love you completely. Thank you for your loyal, godly leadership in our marriage and home. You make "following" a joy and an adventure, and I'm up for whatever the rest of our days look like! xx

To my beautiful generous-hearted children and family: Thank you for cheering me on in every endeavor. . . . I am blessed to be yours and love you so. xx

To our dear, dear Hillsong Church family and friends, pastors and mentors: For many years I have stood in awe of every single part of our church—the past, the present, and the future. Thank you for the joy of being able to do life in a church family. And to our new church family at Hope Unlimited Church . . . we are honored to be called your pastors, and we are believing God for this experience to become the greatest days of our lives.

To the crew at 4B Media and The Hope Office: Deb, Margie, Jared, Caisha, Michelle, and Rachel . . . Andrew, Josh, Markus, and the team at The Grove Studios . . . *wow!* The journey is incredible! Thanks for your willing hearts and your passion to bring answers to human suffering. By God's grace, this is just the beginning.

To the ever-patient Camille and Miffy . . . what do you say to the women who edit you, pray for you, cover you, and make you sound better than you are? Girls, I am forever grateful . . . thank you.

To all our lovely friends: Every day I thank God for you . . . you make my heart smile . . . thanks for your patience. xx

And thank you to Pastor Brian Houston, Pastor Tommy Barnett, Joyce Meyer, Pastor Bill Hybels, John Maxwell, Pastor Jack Hayford, Graham Kendrick, and the many leaders who inspire and input into our lives. Mark and I are eternally grateful.

And thank you, Lord, for saving me, restoring me, and filling my life with a new song to forever declare your worth. All glory, all honor, all power, and all praise to you forever and ever.

Notes

Value One: Time for Growth
1. Robb Report, *Worth* magazine (New York: Sandow Media): Feb. 2004.

Value Two: Encouragement
1. Stuart Garrard, Tim Jupp, Martin Smith, Stewart Smith, and Jon Thatcher, "Our God Reigns" (West Sussex: Curious? Music UK, 2005).
2. John O'Donohue, *Eternal Echoes* (New York: HarperPerennial, 2000), 62.

Value Three: 20/20 Dreams and Visions
1. Henry David Thoreau, *A Week on the Concord and Merrimack Rivers* (New York: Dover, 1849), 149.

Value Four: Energy
1. Chris Tomlin, "God of This City" (Passion Worship Band, 2008).
2. Norman Vincent Peale, *The Power of Positive Thinking* (New York: Ballantine Books, 1982), 35.

Value Five: The Squeeze
1. Peter and Catherine Marshall, *The Prayers of Peter Marshall* (New York: McGraw Hill, 1955).

Value Six: Open Doors
1. Eugene H. Peterson, *A Long Obedience in the Same Direction* (Downers Grove, IL: InterVarsity Press, 2000), 206.
2. John Wesley—statement commonly known as "John Wesley's Rule."

Value Seven: Excellence
1. Oren Harari, *The Powell Principles: 24 Lessons from Colin Powell* (New York: McGraw Hill, 2003), 14.

Value Eight: Humility
1. C. S. Lewis, *Mere Christianity*, revised and amplified ed. (New York: HarperCollins, 2001), 122.
2. Richard Foster, *Celebration of Discipline* (New York: HarperCollins, 1998), 130.

Value Nine: Greater Than Adversity
1. Charles H. Spurgeon, *The Treasury of David*, vol. 2 (New York: Funk & Wagnalls, 1882), 380.
2. S. W. Christophers, *Hymn-Writers and Their Hymns.* Words by Martin Luther (London: S. W. Partridge & Co., 1866), 11.

Value Twelve: People
1. Arthur P. Stanley, *Historical Memorials of Canterbury.* Quote from Augustine (London: John Murray, 1883).

Value Thirteen: Genius
1. Gene Weingarten, "Pearls Before Breakfast," *Washington Post*, April 8, 2007.

Value Fourteen: Hearts of Flesh
1. Paul O'Rourke, *Blessings of the Poor* (Sydney, Australia: Strand Publishing, 2007).
2. Anne Frank, *Diary of a Young Girl* (New York: Doubleday, 1952).

Finale: A Study of Devotion
1. Richard Foster, *Celebration of Discipline* (New York: HarperCollins, 1998), 159.

HOPE:Rwanda

HOPE is a faith-based, non-profit organization that brings together church, government, NGO's, private enterprise, healthcare and individuals, to provide practical solutions to countries devastated by war, genocide and poverty.

Our primary objective is to assist developing nations reduce poverty, achieve sustainable development, and to bring spiritual strength and social justice to every segment of society.

How are we bringing HOPE?

- Village of Hope: a purpose-built community caring for widows and orphans in Rwanda.
- Education: strengthening tens of thousands of teachers through professional development training in Rwanda, Uganda, Kenya and Cambodia.
- Poverty reduction: community based micro-enterprise development & business mentoring.

www.hoperwanda.org

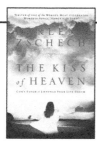